On Silencing

On Silencing

What It Is and Why It Matters

MARY KATE McGOWAN

OXFORD
UNIVERSITY PRESS

OXFORD
UNIVERSITY PRESS

Oxford University Press is a department of the University of Oxford.
It furthers the University's objective of excellence in research, scholarship,
and education by publishing worldwide. Oxford is a registered trade mark of
Oxford University Press in the UK and in certain other countries.

Published in the United States of America by Oxford University Press
198 Madison Avenue, New York, NY 10016, United States of America.

CIP data is on file at the Library of Congress

ISBN 9780197837290

DOI: 10.1093/9780197837320.001.0001

Printed by Integrated Books International, United States of America

The manufacturer's authorized representative in the EU for product safety is
Oxford University Press España S.A. of Parque Empresarial San Fernando de Henares,
Avenida de Castilla, 2 – 28830 Madrid (www.oup.es/en or product.safety@oup.com).
OUP España S.A. also acts as importer into Spain of products made by the manufacturer.

Contents

Acknowledgments

This book has been years in the making, and there are many to thank for their help along the way. I thank all the participants in the University of Cambridge Speech and Normativity Workshop who gave feedback on a very early draft. In particular, I thank Claudia Bianchi, Quill Kukla, Maciej Witek, Nero Marsili, Marelene Valek, Rae Langton, Bianca Ceppollaro, Marcin Lewinski, Lucy McDonald, Laura Valentini, Steve Oswald, and most especially Laura Caponetto for organizing the workshop and for including me in it. I thank the brilliant and intellectually curious Wellesley students in the first iteration of PHIL 318 (Silencing). They are Alex Asack, Rachel Fei, Sarah Geist, Selale Gunal, Wren Hager, C.J. Jin, Mira Kumar, Pace Li, Michelle Lim, Carrington Parks, Taylor Quaye, Bridget Sheng, Adeline van Buskirk, and Phoebe Weisiger-Vallas. The book is richer for their explorations and prodding. I thank my honors theses and independent study students who dug down on related topics with me. They are Rachel Fei, Taylor Quaye, and Edilia Foster. I am grateful to my editor at Oxford University Press, Peter Ohlin, whose no-nonsense support of this project helped to carry it through. I also thank reviewers for both Oxford University Press and Princeton University Press who offered illuminating feedback, most especially the (otherwise dreaded) reviewer 2 for Princeton who offered particularly thorough, generous, insightful, appreciative, and constructive suggestions. I also thank Yixi Gao and Lenox Balzebre, two intrepid Wellesley first-years, for going over the manuscript with a fine-toothed comb this past summer and catching many things I had missed. I am grateful to Ishani Maitra and Veronika Fuechtner for insightful feedback on the silencing chapter in *Words in Action*. This book also benefited immensely from their expertise. I thank Phoebe Weisiger-Vallas for her insight and meticulous care in helping to assemble the index. I thank Wellesley College for supporting my research, valuing feminist scholarship well before it was mainstreamed in my discipline, and affording me the opportunity to teach such amazing students. I am grateful to Jennifer Hornsby and Rae Langton who got this whole conversation started—in analytic philosophy anyway. I am especially thankful to Rae, whose work sparked my foray into the social philosophy of language, reinvigorating my love for philosophy and occupying my research interests for the past almost 30 years. My debt to Rae is immense. Finally and foremost, I thank my family. They keep me afloat.

To Shea and Nora. Your names make it into many examples in this book I am unspeakably proud of the humans you have become.

1

An Overview

Lately, there has been quite a lot of discussion—both in academic philosophy and in the media—about silencing. It is alleged to be an affront to free speech, a violation of individual freedom, a mechanism of social inequality, an enemy to a well-functioning democracy, and spreading like wildfire. If these claims are true, then silencing is an important phenomenon that really needs to be properly understood. That much is clear. Other things are, however, significantly less clear: What is silencing exactly? Why does it matter? What precisely is bad about it, if indeed it is bad? And, what ought to be done in response to it?

This book will address these questions but it will not provide single answers to them. Much will be left open and this is deliberate. Rather than try to settle every pertinent question, *On Silencing* aims instead to provide a framework for thinking through the complexities for oneself. And, another main aim of the book is to show just how complex these issues really are. Quick assessments, knee jerk reactions, and pat answers have no place in discussions about how a person's ability to communicate can be impaired in the very messy and all-too-real real world.

§ 1.1 What Is Silencing?

Let's first think about what silencing is. Different sorts of claims have been made. Pornography is alleged to silence women and the liberal climate on college campuses is alleged to silence

On Silencing. Mary Kate McGowan, Oxford University Press. © Mary Kate McGowan 2026.
DOI: 10.1093/9780197837320.003.0001

conservative voices.[1] At first glance anyway, these claims seem quite different. The first claim, the one about pornography, seems to involve the claim that pornography consumption causes women to be viewed in ways that lead to their being misunderstood. On this way of thinking, pornography causes, for example, women's sincere sexual refusals to be misinterpreted as something else (as insincere, coy, or mere role playing). If this is silencing, then silencing appears to be a kind of misinterpretation, a mistake that results in miscommunication.

The claim about liberal campuses seems different. Although it certainly could involve being misunderstood, it seems more concerned with being unjustly punished for voicing unpopular views. The worry here is that conservatives are sometimes vilified when they do express their views and, as a result, conservatives on university campuses become extremely reluctant to say what they think. If true, this is bad; it would undermine healthy debate and go directly against the very mission of higher education. If this is silencing, then it seems to be concerned with the consequences of being understood: either being punished for communicating one's views or being prevented from doing so out of fear of that punishment. Here, the issue is not miscommunication, but the punishing effects of successful communication.

These two examples suggest that there is a lot going on here and silencing might be more than one thing. In short, that's right. As we shall see, silencing can manifest in a variety of different forms. For further evidence of this, consider the following cases[2]:

Soundproof Box: A stressed out and desperate father, Michael, finds himself unable to tolerate the relentless banter of his high-energy three-year old son, Johnny. So, whenever Michael really needs some headspace, he lovingly places little Johnny inside a small but cozy sound proof box that Michael built for this very purpose.

Duct Tape: Joe is robbing Margot; concerned that she might scream and alert her neighbors, Joe places duct tape on her mouth.

Refusing Help: Cindy says, "No, really, thank you but it's important to me to do this myself; I can do it and I would not want to trouble you unnecessarily," in order to politely decline Carl's generous offer of help. Unable to shake his view of women as damsels in distress, Carl interprets Cindy as politely accepting his help.

No Police Report: Linda is an African American woman who experiences domestic abuse. She decides against reporting it to the police because she fears that the only result of doing so would be to reinforce the stereotype, already present in the minds of the police and society at large, that Black men are violent.[3]

Woman Boss: Jane is the boss but when she orders her employees to do things, they tend to interpret her as issuing requests. When they do what she asks, they resent her failure to thank them properly and so they think she's a rude incompetent boss.[4]

Dismissed Witness: Claire is an unhoused person who witnesses a street crime; she testifies at trial but the jury dismisses her testimony. Presumably because she is unhoused, they judge her to be without credibility.[5]

In each of these cases something goes wrong with communication but different things seem to go wrong in each of these cases. Little Johnny, for example, is not prevented from speaking but he is prevented from being heard. Margot is prevented from speaking or screaming. Cindy is able to speak but her utterance is misunderstood; she is refusing but her refusal is mistaken for an acceptance. Linda, on the other hand, decides against speaking because her audience is affected by harmful stereotypes that would alter how her words are taken. Jane's orders are mistaken for requests, and Claire is understood perfectly well. It's just that her testimony is given less credibility than it ought to be given.

Despite these differences, each of these cases involve a speaker's ability to communicate being undermined in some way. In light of this, it makes sense to treat silencing as a primarily communicative phenomenon. In fact, the characterization of silencing that I identify in Chapter 3 focuses on (various kinds of) communicative failure. Since we aim, in this book, to explore silencing in its many forms, we really need, at the very outset, to be as clear as possible about what it is. For this reason, our first task is to more carefully spell out a working definition of silencing. In that chapter, we will also explore some of the issues that arise when doing so.

As we have already seen, silencing takes many forms. Another thing I will do in this book is distinguish between and then explore several different kinds.[6]

One type involves a speaker trying to communicate something, but the addressee (who is the person being spoken to) fails to recognize an important aspect of that intended communication. If something interferes with the addressee's recognition, then the speaker is silenced because their attempt to communicate is thwarted; something gets in the way of successful communication. Different sorts of recognition failures are possible. An addressee might correctly interpret the meaning or content of what is being said but mistake, say, an order for a request. This is what happens in *Woman Boss* where Jane's order is mistaken for a (mere) request. Another possibility involves a failure to recognize the speaker's authority or standing to perform the speech action in question. For example, if Sally orders Steve but Steve doesn't realize that Sally has the authority to do so, then Steve will take her utterance as a failed attempt to order him. Although Steve recognizes Sally's intention to order him, he nevertheless thinks her order fails. Yet another option involves an addressee mistaking a sincere utterance for an insincere one. So another way that an attempted communication can go awry is if Steve were to mistake Sally's sincere order for an insincere one. We will explore these sorts of cases in *Chapter 4: You Got That Wrong: On Varieties of Miscommunication.*

There is also the possibility of silencing happening later, after communication succeeds. Another version of communicative failure concerns the impact of a communication being improperly prevented. If, for example, an utterance is prevented from having the effect in the world that it ought to have, then the speaker is silenced in a different way. Claims that are given less credibility than they should be given, as in *Dismissed Witness*, or orders that are not obeyed, and refusals that are not respected, are each potential examples of this form of silencing. This kind of impact prevention is explored in *Chapter 5: Ineffectual Words: On Impact Prevention.*

Yet another type of silencing occurs before communication is even attempted. This can happen in a variety of ways. A speaker might be physically prevented from speaking, as in *Duct Tape*, or prohibited from doing so. Another possibility might be called 'self-silencing'. It involves a speaker deciding against speaking. The conditions under which a decision to remain silent ought to count as silencing are complex, subtle, and in need of clarification. One way that this can happen is when a speaker anticipates that her words will cause harm and the harm results because of mistakes made by her audience. *No Police Report* is a potential example of this type. Here, the speaker is aware that her audience is affected by stereotypes that will cause them to overgeneralize in a harmful way. This broad type of silencing is discussed in *Chapter 6: Not Saying That: On Preventing Communication Attempts.*

Defining silencing and exploring its different forms is distinct from identifying what makes it happen. What causes silencing? Which social forces contribute to it? A complete answer to this question is well beyond the scope of this little book; I cannot possibly identify everything that contributes to communication being undermined. Instead, in *Chapter 7: On Complex Contributors,* I explore three phenomena and consider their connection to silencing. In particular, we shall see that they each cause each of the three types of silencing. And, this is why they are called 'complex contributors'.

§ 1.2   Why Care?

So why should one care about silencing, understood as communicative failure? As we shall see in more detail throughout the book, there are several reasons.

First, silencing can harm individual speakers. If a person's communicative capacities are undermined, so is that person's autonomy and capacity for self-expression, their ability to navigate the social world, contribute to shared knowledge, and participate in political deliberation. And, when silencing is systematic, that is, when there are widespread social group-based structural barriers to successful communication, we have even more reason to care.

There are also potential social effects. After all, if speakers are disabled, then we all lose. If credible speakers are treated as less credible than they should be, our collective quest for knowledge is undermined so, as a knowledge community, we are worse off. There are considerable consequences for democracy too. The ability to communicate is central to a well-functioning democracy; we need to be able to tell our representatives what we think; we need to be able to collectively deliberate about matters of public concern. If, however, our ability to successfully communicate is undermined, then to the extent that communication is thwarted so too is the deliberative process at the center of our democracy. Moreover, if silencing is group-based (that is, if it happens to people because of their marginalized social status), then these effects will be amplified and so too should our concern about, and attention to, them.

One of the main themes of this book is the inferential nature of communication. We have to figure out what a speaker means by what that speaker says. After all, what a person literally says is usually distinct from what they mean in saying it. To see this, consider the following.

Sarcasm: Shea and Nora are waiting in a very long line at a grocery store when Nora turns to Shea and says "Well, now, this is fun."

What Nora literally says ('Well, now, this is fun') is distinct from what she means to convey on this occasion (namely, something like 'This is the opposite of fun'). Here, Shea has to figure this out. Shea infers Nora's intended meaning from what Nora actually says along with a whole lot of other information: the context in which she says it, her tone of voice, her facial expression, and emotional state; Shea will rely on background information about what is and what is not fun or regarded as fun; he will also tap into what he believes Nora believes and—even more complex—Shea will rely on what he believes Nora believes that he believes. This is because when Nora decides what to actually say to convey what she means, she relies on what she thinks Shea will be able to figure out; for this reason, Nora also relies on what she believes Shea believes.

Despite these complexities, this case is pretty simple: Nora means the opposite of what she actually says and the context makes this pretty darn clear. That said, this case does highlight both that communication is inferential and that the inferences involved rely on a whole host of additional—hopefully shared—information. Given this, it is fairly surprising that we manage to communicate successfully as often as we do. Setting that aside for a moment, a consideration of this case also shows how many ways there are for things to go wrong. We can misinterpret a facial expression, tone, or emotional state and we are more likely to do so when we are interacting with someone who is previously unknown to us or somehow different from us. We can also be mistaken in our assumptions about what information is assumed, shared, or relevant. And, again, we are more likely to make errors about these things when we are interacting with someone who is new to us or different from us. All of this is to say that we should always be aware of the possibility of these errors and we should be even more careful, both as speakers and as hearers, when we are trying to communicate across difference.

This humility and need for care is warranted in communicative situations involving all sorts of difference. Most of us realize, for example, that we should try a little harder when communicating with someone from another culture but we should also be sensitive to the possibility of communication-undermining differences when speaking with people from other regions, socio-economic levels, genders, races, and political affiliations. All of these differences can affect how speakers signal what they mean and what background information is taken for granted. So, before you decide that someone is wrong, or stupid, or brainwashed, or over-sensitive, or evil, or selfish, or callous, consider first the possibility that you've gotten something wrong. A little humility can go a long way, especially in such a multiply polarized environment.

§ 1.3 The Audiences

This book is written for two audiences. First and foremost, it is written to be accessible to a more general audience, that is, for everyone. One need not be an academic philosopher or any kind of professor to be interested in, and to understand, this book. *On Silencing* aims to explain what silencing is, why it matters, how it manifests, what brings it about, and what we can do in response to it; and, it aims to do these things *without* assuming any prior technical knowledge. In particular, this means that any necessary background is spelled out and unnecessary complexities and details are glossed over.

That said, *On Silencing* also contributes new material to academic discussions about silencing; it isn't "just" making those debates accessible to non-experts. For this reason, academics who work on silencing are also a target audience. In fact, each of the main chapters of the book adds new developments to the growing academic literature on silencing. And, this new material is rolled out in a way that is available to all readers.

§ 1.4 The Contents

Here is a brief overview of the book. In Chapter 2, I introduce the main tools from the philosophy of language that I will need. The inferential nature of communication and the basics of speech act theory are presented there. Then, in Chapter 3, I define silencing, as involving communicative failure, and I consider several issues about how to define it. I will also identify three different senses of communicative failure, a strict one, one concerning impact, and another concerning attempt prevention. In Chapter 4, I explore the miscommunication type of silencing. Here, a communication attempt is made but some aspect of that communication is not properly recognized. As we shall see, there are many different recognition failures possible. This chapter discusses several of them and then explores whether they should count as silencing. In Chapter 5, I turn my attention to a different candidate type of silencing. These are cases where communication succeeds but it is prevented from having the impact that it ought to have. There too there are many different ways that speech can impact the world and also many ways for those impacts to be prevented. Which ones should count as silencing and why will also be explored. Chapter 6 considers cases where a communication attempt is prevented altogether. This can happen for a whole host of different reasons and only some of them will count as silencing. I will also consider cases where speakers decide against speaking. Again, there are many different reasons why a person might refrain from saying something; I will identify what I call harm prevention self-silencing and argue that such cases should count as silencing. Finally, in the last chapter, I consider what I call complex contributors to silencing, phenomena that contribute to all of the three identified broad types of silencing; I also explore several interesting cases.

So, let's get started. I turn now to the task of describing the language tools that I will need in this investigation.

2

Understanding Language Use

This book is about silencing and, although I will give a more precise characterization of silencing in the next chapter, we already know that it involves problems with communication. Thus, in order to understand silencing, it makes sense to first get a better grip on how communication works. The idea is this: only once we understand how communication works, when it works well, can we see the various ways that communication can go wrong.

§ 2.1 Cases of Non-linguistic Communication

Language is the main way that we communicate, but it is not the only way. We can tell people things without using words. Here are some examples:

Caught in the Act: Sam is a middle school student who loves to play video games. His parents have imposed a household rule prohibiting him from playing these games until after 7:00 p.m. His mom enters his room one afternoon, sees him playing Fortnite, and proceeds to stare him down while she arches her right eyebrow knowingly. She doesn't say a word. She doesn't have to.

Boring Class: In a high school class of 28 students, the teacher has been talking non-stop about elements, substances, compounds, and mixtures for the past 20 minutes. One student, Greg, turns to Jane, the student to his left, and rolls his eyes. Greg does not say a word but his message is clear.

On Silencing. Mary Kate McGowan, Oxford University Press. © Mary Kate McGowan 2026.
DOI: 10.1093/9780197837320.003.0002

Political Expression: Jill, a liberal Democrat, and a huge fan of Ruth Bader Ginsberg, stands outside a voting center wearing a black robe, large eyeglasses, and a lace collar. She holds no sign but her political affiliations are perfectly clear.

In each of these cases, someone manages to communicate perfectly well even though that person does not use language to do so. The mom, in *Caught in the Act*, lets her son know that she knows he broke the rule and that he will be held accountable for doing so. Arguably, her stare down relays that message better than any words could. Similarly, in *Boring Class*, Greg makes his sentiments perfectly clear even though Greg is utterly silent. Greg means something with his eye roll and Jane knows exactly what that is. Finally, in *Political Expression*, Jill expresses her political affiliation through her attire and not through anything she actually says. In each of these cases then, a person communicates perfectly well and that person does so without using words at all.

In the next few sections, I will identify important characteristics of communication. Again, by making them explicit, we will be better able to understand ways that communication can go awry.

§ 2.2 Communication Is Intentional

The picture of communication that is emerging here is an intentional one. This means that when a person communicates something, that person intends to communicate that thing. Had Greg rolled his eyes because a mosquito flew into it and he was just trying to get the mosquito out, then his eye roll action would not be a communicative act. This is so even if someone else interpreted Greg's eye roll as a communicative act and even if it was perfectly reasonable for that person to do so. On this view of communication then, the speaker's intention to communicate the message in question is absolutely necessary for it to be a real instance of communication (as opposed to being reasonably mistaken for one).

There is another broader view of communication and it's worth considering it now so I can distinguish it from the intentional notion of communication that is my present focus in this book. Consider the following examples.

Dark Clouds: Rose sees dark clouds on the horizon and realizes that a storm is coming.

Tennis Outfit: Hudson sees his neighbor, Karen, in the supermarket. Because Karen is wearing a tennis outfit, Hudson realizes that Karen plays tennis.

In each of these cases, there is a sense in which something is "communicated". In *Dark Clouds*, for example, the clouds communicate to Rose that bad weather is imminent and, in *Tennis Outfit*, Karen's outfit communicates to Hudson that Karen is a tennis player. Notice first that this notion of communication is not intentional; that would require that the communication sender intends to send the message in question and, in these cases, this is not what is happening. Dark clouds in the sky are not trying to tell Rose anything; clouds have no minds and thus no intentions. Similarly, telling Hudson (or anyone) that she is a tennis player is not something that Karen is trying to get across. Unlike Jill in *Political Expression*, Karen's attire isn't chosen in order to communicate a message. She's just dressed that way because she is headed to the gym after she picks up her groceries.

In each of these cases, what is "communicated" is something that is reasonably inferred. The presence of dark clouds can be a very good indicator that a storm is coming and a person wearing a tennis outfit is quite good evidence that that person plays tennis. Although this notion of communication is a perfectly legitimate one, it is not the notion of communication that concerns me here. In this book, I am concerned with the *intentional* notion of communication.

It's worthwhile to pause here and consider the nature of this intention.[1] It's called the communicative intention and it's got a complex structure. It involves an intention *and* an intention about that intention (which is called a *meta-intention*). In *Boring Class*, when Greg communicated his annoyance to Jane about the boring chemistry class, he both intended to communicate this message *and* he intended for Jane to recognize that intention. That is, he intended to communicate something to Jane and he intended to communicate that thing to Jane through Jane's recognition of his intention to communicate it to her. This meta-intention is the core of communication but it's probably easier to see this meta-intention—and why it matters—by considering a case where it's missing. To this end, consider the following case.

> *Cool Kid*: Whitney just transferred to a new school and she desperately wants her new schoolmates to think that she was super popular at her old school so she joins a listserv so that her phone is constantly binging as if she is receiving texts from old school chums.

In *Cool Kid*, Whiney intends for her classmates to infer that she was popular at her old school so it might seem like a clear case of communication but really it is not. This is because the meta-intention is missing. Although Whitney intends for her new classmates to believe that she was popular, she definitely does not want them to realize that she intends for them to come to believe this. Whitney's intention is not a communicative intention because it lacks the required meta-intention.

To drive the point home, consider Greg again. When he rolls his eyes, he intends to communicate that he is bored *and* he wants this recognized. That is, Greg wants to get something across and he wants to get it across in a fairly specific way—namely via the recognition of his intention to get it across. That's the meta-intention and it's crucial for communication, in this sense.

§ 2.3 Communication Is Inferential

Communication is also inferential. This means that, to a certain extent anyway, people have to figure out what is being communicated. In each of the cases of communication discussed above, the intended message is figured out or inferred. Although it is probably not at all difficult for Sam to suss out, his mom's message in *Caught in the Act* is nevertheless something Sam has to infer. Moreover, doing so requires access to shared background information. Sam is able to access his mother's intended meaning because they both know (and they both know that they both know) that he is not supposed to be playing video games during the day; she can see that he is playing Fortnite; Fortnite is a video game; his mom raises her eyebrow when she is angry, and so forth. Even though the communicated meaning is pretty obvious in this case, it's still inferred and it is inferred so easily because the requisite background information is shared between the two of them.

So far, I have focused on cases of communication that do not involve language. It is now time to turn to language use as a vehicle for communication.

One might think, however, that once we use words to communicate, those words will convey the intended meaning; and, since accessing the intended meaning just requires understanding what is said, linguistic communication need not require such complex inferences. I call this the decoding model of speech and it's worth investigating.

According to this model, when a speaker wants to communicate something, the speaker says something that literally means that very thing. A hearer figures out what the speaker means by interpreting the literal meaning of what the speaker actually says. (We shall continue to call the receivers and interpreters of language 'hearers' even though this term is not without its issues.[2]) Here, communication is just a matter of coding and decoding the content of what the speaker wants to communicate. This picture of language use makes a lot of sense. After all, we use language to communicate what we mean and we say (or write) things that have meaning, so it seems reasonable to expect that what we say (or write) should match the meaning we intend to convey.

As intuitive as this picture maybe, it's not accurate. As a matter of fact, we rarely say what we intend to get across. Instead, we say something *else* that enables the hearer to figure out what we intend to get across. This kind of intended and inferred meaning is called an 'implicature'.[3] To see an example of this, consider the following case.

Statin Implicature: Piotra and Newt are talking about how confused and forgetful their father has been lately, when Piotra says, "Lots of statin medications have neurological side effects".

In this case, Newt takes Piotra to be telling him that their dad's forgetfulness and confusion are being caused by the statin medication that he is currently taking. Although this is exactly what Piotra intends to communicate to Newt, it is not what she actually says. What Piotra actually says is a general claim about statin medications; it is not a claim about their father at all. Despite this, Newt is able to figure out Piotra's intended meaning easily enough; he is able to do this because he combines what she actually says, along with facts about the context, the cooperative nature of conversation, and good old common sense.

On this inferential picture of linguistic communication, the meaning of what the speaker actually says is just a really helpful *clue* about what the speaker is trying to get across. In *Statin Implicature*, Piotra said something that enabled Newt to figure out what she meant. Similarly in *Political Expression*, Jill's clothing and glasses are a helpful communicative clue and others are able to decipher what Jill means to get across. On this inferential picture of communication then, what is actually said is a helpful clue about what is meant; it is not a translation of what is meant (as the decoding picture would have it).

That we often mean something different from what we say draws our attention to an important distinction between conventional meaning, on the one hand, and speaker meaning, on the other. What Piotra means by what she says (her speaker meaning) is clearly distinct from the conventional meaning of what she actually says. Piotra's speaker meaning is something like: our father's recent forgetfulness and confusion are being caused by the statin medication that he is taking. This is also what Newt takes her to be telling him. The conventional meaning of Piotra's utterance, by contrast, is the literal meaning of what she actually says: Lots of statin medications have neurological side effects.

Irony provides another familiar illustration of this contrast between speaker meaning and conventional meaning.

Irony: Having eaten the entire large pizza within minutes and with evident relish, Jim delicately wipes his greasy mouth with a napkin and declares, "I don't like pizza; never touch the stuff".

What Jim means here (among other things) is that he obviously really loves pizza. What his words actually mean (that is, the conventional, as opposed to the speaker, meaning of his utterance) is that he doesn't like pizza and he never eats it. Again, speaker meaning, or what the speaker means by what he says, is distinct from the conventional meaning of the words actually used. When a speaker is being ironic, the speaker meaning is the exact opposite of the conventional meaning of what is said.

We have now considered several examples where the speaker's intended meaning is distinct from what the speaker actually says but the speaker meaning is nevertheless communicated successfully because the hearer recognizes it. In other words, the hearer figured out—or successfully inferred—what the speaker intended to get across.

Now, one might think that speaker meaning is inferred in this way but the conventional meaning is straightforwardly decoded. As we shall now see, it's quite a bit more complicated than that. Even direct literal language use (where the speaker says exactly what she means) involves complex inferential reasoning.

> *Tall Peter*: Charles says, "Peter is tall". Charles means to convey that Peter is tall and he is not insinuating that anything else is true of Peter.

In *Tall Peter*, Charles's speaker meaning matches the conventional meaning of what he says. Even here, however, hearers must make rather complex inferences to correctly interpret the meaning of what Charles says. For starters, they need to figure out which person Charles is talking about. Lots of people are named 'Peter' but Charles's claim pertains to exactly one of them. Furthermore, hearers also need to figure out what constitutes being tall for someone like Peter. If Peter is a professional basketball player, for example, then saying that he is tall probably means that he is over seven feet. If, however, Peter is a preschooler, then it means no such thing.

So, communication is inferential. Hearers have to figure out what speakers mean and this is true of both conventional meaning and speaker meaning.

§ 2.4 Communication Is Cooperative

Linguistic communication is also cooperative.[4] This means that when we use words to communicate, we ought to say something that enables the other person to figure out what we mean. In *Statin Implicature*, for example, what Piotra meant was different from what she said but what she said enabled Newt to easily figure out what she meant. Piotra was being cooperative. In all the cases of communication we have thus far considered, the speaker was being cooperative in this sense. In *Boring Class*, for example, Greg's eye roll enabled Jane to easily figure out what Greg meant. Greg was being communicatively cooperative.

Those on the receiving end of linguistic communication need to be cooperative too.[5] That hearers should be cooperative means that they should make a good faith effort to correctly identify what the speaker means. As hearers, we have a job to do and we ought to aim to get it right. By figuring out what Piotra meant, Newt was being cooperative. Communication is a two-way street; so is the cooperation it relies on.

That communication is cooperative in *this* sense does not mean that it is cooperative in every sense. Successful cases of communication can involve all sorts of problematic "uncooperative" behavior but these cases of successful communication still involve the relevant kind of *communicative cooperation*. This is tricky and subtle so some examples are in order.

> *Withholding Information*: Ken bought Sam a birthday present and Sam wants to know what it is. A week before Sam's birthday and in response to Sam's request that Ken tell him what the present is, Ken says "You'll just have to wait".

> *Lying*: Dan ate Kate's chocolate bar. When Kate asks Dan if he knows what happened to it, Dan responds, "I have no idea what happened to your chocolate bar".

> *Feigning Misunderstanding*: Aoife tells her work colleague that she loves to set dance[6]; he pretends to mishear her and goes on at great length about how much he would enjoy watching her sex dance.

In each of these cases, there is a sense in which the speaker or hearer is being uncooperative. In *Withholding Information*, for example, Ken is uncooperative in a sense because he has information that Sam wants and yet Ken is refusing to provide it. In *Lying*,

Dan is being uncooperative because he is lying and, in *Feigning Misunderstanding*, Aoife's work colleague is being uncooperative because he is pretending to misunderstand what she said (and he might well be doing so in order to harass her).

Even so, in each of these cases, the speaker (or hearer) is being communicatively cooperative. In both *Withholding Information* and *Lying*, for example, the speaker is being communicatively cooperative because what the speaker says enables the hearer to figure out what the speaker means by what they say. In *Withholding Information*, for example, Ken means to tell Sam that Ken is not going to tell Sam what the present is before Sam's birthday and what Ken says (e.g., "You'll just have to wait") enables Sam to figure this out. Thus although Ken is not giving Sam the information that Sam requested and Ken is being uncooperative in *that* sense, Ken is nevertheless communicatively cooperative. In *Lying*, Dan intends to communicate to Kate that he did not eat the chocolate and he does not know who did and what Dan says enables Kate to infer this. Now, what Dan intends to get across is a lie but Dan is nevertheless communicatively cooperative because what he says enables Kate to access the intended (albeit known to be false) content. Finally, in *Feigning Misunderstanding*, it is the hearer's cooperation at issue. Here, the co-worker correctly identifies what Aoife said; he had no problem correctly identifying her intended meaning; it's just that he pretends not to. As these cases illustrate, successful communication requires cooperation from both the speaker and the hearer but it requires only this minimal kind of communicative cooperation.

§ 2.5 Communication Is Context-Sensitive

Finally, communication is highly context-sensitive. Both what an utterance means (so the conventional meaning) and what a speaker means by an utterance (so the speaker meaning) varies from context to context. We will be seeing this context sensitivity throughout the book, so a few simple examples will suffice for now. Consider Charles's uttering of "Peter is tall" in *Tall Peter*. If this is said during an NBA commentary about a professional basketball player named Peter, it means something very different than it would if said about a five-year-old child named 'Peter'. Here, the meaning of what is said changes across the contexts. This is both because the referent of the name 'Peter' changes and because the relevant standards of tallness change.

Speaker meaning also varies across contexts and this really shouldn't be surprising. After all, speaker meaning is determined by the speaker's communicative intentions and what a speaker wants to get across will vary between contexts. It's worth stressing, though, that the very same string of words can help to communicate very different speaker meanings. To see this, consider someone saying, "I'd love that". If this is said in response to a dinner invitation, it means one thing. If, instead, it is said in response to a prediction that that person's political party will win by a landslide, it means quite another. The context sensitivity of language use is both pervasive and complex. We will be seeing it again and again.

Thus far, we have seen that communication is intentional, inferential, cooperative, and context-sensitive. So far, though, we have only been focusing on a part of what language use does: the communication of content. As we shall see in the next section, language use does a whole lot more besides that.

§ 2.6 Speech Acts: It's Not Just Content

We can also *do things* with words. We can apologize, place a bet, enact a law, undertake a promise, or issue an order. Language use is not just in the business of communicating true or false claims; it's not just about communicating content.

J.L. Austin, the philosopher who first drew our philosophical attention to this action-like role of language use, introduced a few distinctions that I will be relying on.[7] According to Austin, when we use language, our utterance has several forces. First, the *locutionary* force of an utterance is roughly the conventional content; it's the meaning of what is actually said about the things being referred to. When Dmitri tells John, "There is a fire on Cypress Street," Dmitri's utterance has locutionary force since Dmitri uttered words that have specific meaning and reference. Although there may be many streets in the universe named Cypress, Dmitri's particular use of this name on this occasion refers to a particular street.

Second, the *illocutionary* force of an utterance is the action constituted by the utterance in virtue of the utterance functioning as speech. Although the physical production of speech (whether written, verbal, or signed) is an action, it is not an illocutionary act. The illocutionary act is performed by means of the locutionary act of expressing content. So, when Dmitri said, "There is a fire on Cypress Street," he thereby asserted (and thus committed himself to the truth of) the claim that there is a fire on Cypress Street; he might also have been warning others that there is a fire on Cypress Street. Other illocutionary acts include ordering (e.g., "I order you to finish the report by Friday"), apologizing (e.g., "I apologize for eating your dessert while your head was turned"), and promising (e.g., "Yes, mom, I promise to wash the dishes every night after dinner").

Third and finally, the *perlocutionary* force of an utterance is a certain sort of causal effect on the audience. In order for a causal effect to be a perlocutionary effect, it must be brought about by means of the linguistic functioning of the utterance. In other words, non-linguistic causal effects of speech (such as a shrill voice breaking glass or a loud announcement waking someone) are not perlocutionary effects since these causal effects are not brought about by means of the hearer's recognition of the conventional meaning of the words uttered. Perlocutionary effects are thus a subset of causal effects. When Dmitri said 'There is a fire on Cypress Street', his assertion is likely to change hearers' beliefs. Typically, hearers will come to believe that what Dmitri said is true, and so they will come to believe that there is a fire on Cypress Street.[8] Suppose now that Dmitri's utterance is also a warning. Warnings also have perlocutionary effects; in particular, they strive to change hearers' beliefs about relevant dangers, and they also seek to change what hearers do.

Typically, there is a particular perlocutionary effect that the speaker hopes to bring about via their utterance. When Dmitri said that there is a fire on Cypress Street, he aimed to inform others and thereby prevent them from exposing themselves to a potentially dangerous situation. Causing his hearers to avoid these dangers are perlocutionary effects of Dmitri's warning. Other perlocutionary effects include convincing, alarming, persuading, scaring, amusing, and inspiring.

With these distinctions in hand, we can already see quite a few ways that an utterance can go wrong. At the locutionary level, a hearer might mishear what a person actually says (as the co-worker pretended to do in *Feigning Misunderstanding*); a hearer can genuinely mishear or misunderstand the content of what is said, or a hearer can correctly identify the conventional meaning but misidentify the intended speaker meaning.

At the illocutionary level, an order can be mistaken for a prediction, a warning can be taken as a threat, and a refusal treated as consent. Let's make this concrete with some examples.

Clean Room: A harried mother orders her teenage son to clean his cataclysmic room when she says, "You'd better clean that room by the time I get home from work or you'll regret it". Given his quirky cognitive profile, the son sincerely takes her to be predicting how he will feel if he does not clean his room before she gets home. Doubting her prediction, he spends the day playing video games.

Break Up: During their 7-year relationship, Stacy meticulously managed Rick's complex medical situation. Just as they decided to part for good, Stacy says. "I hope you're sure about this. If you leave me, your health will take a serious turn for the worse". In saying this, Stacy intends to warn Rick about what will happen without her careful management of his health, but Rick takes it as a threat.

In each of these cases, the hearer understands what the speaker has said and roughly what she means in saying it; it's just that they each misunderstand what sort of speech action (illocution) the speaker is performing. In *Clean Room*, the son mistakes his mother's order for a mere prediction and, in *Break Up*, Rick interprets Stacy's prediction as a threat.

Things can also go awry at the perlocutionary level as when assertions are not believed, orders are not followed, and refusals are not respected. Suppose that no one believes Dmitri about the fire on Cypress Street. In such a case, his assertion does not bring about its intended perlocutionary effects. Suppose Tim realizes that Paul is refusing to share his cupcake with him, but Tim takes a big chunk of it anyway. In this case, Paul's refusal is not respected; its aim of stopping Tim is not achieved.

Although I shall have much more to say about the various possibilities throughout the book, an appreciation of the complexity of language use already illuminates quite a few quite different potential problems.

Before I move on, one last distinction from Austin. Sometimes, when something goes wrong with a speech act, the attempted illocutionary act fails; the defect is a fatal one; Austin calls such cases *misfires*. Here are some examples:

Indignant Toddler: Precocious three-year-old Catherine wants a lollipop so she tries to order her mother to buy her one. Catherine says, "Because I am your kid you have to do what I say and I say you have to buy me that lollipop!"

Toaster Apology: Dave's eyesight is really failing and, mistaking his toaster for his wife, he turns to the toaster and says, "I'm so sorry I insulted your parents. You know I love them even though they are liberal".

In each of these cases, something has gone wrong. In *Indignant Toddler,* the speaker, Catherine, does not have the authority to perform the intended illocution. Assuming that having authority is necessary for ordering, Catherine tries to order her mother but she fails to do so exactly because she lacks that authority. Something goes wrong in *Toaster Apology* too. Here, the speaker is mistaken about whom (or what) he is addressing. Assuming that one cannot apologize to one's wife by saying something to a toaster, Dave's utterance misfires and, as a result, it fails to be an apology at all.

Other defects, by contrast, are non-fatal. These sorts of defects do not prevent the speech act from having the intended illocutionary force. Here are some examples.

Insincere Promise: Jeanne borrows Dean's car and when she says, "Thank you so much, Dean, I promise to return it with a full tank of gas," she has no intention of filling the tank.

Fickle Groom: Matt marries Anna at an elaborate ceremony in New York. When Matt meets Anna's attractive college roommate, Kendall, at the reception, Matt decides to leave Anna for Kendall.

In these cases too something is not as it should be but the defect in question does not prevent the utterance from having the intended illocutionary force. In *Insincere Promise*, for example, even though Jeanne does not intend to keep the promise (as she certainly should), Jeanne still intends to promise. Since Jeanne intends to undertake an obligation to fill the tank (even though she does not intend to respect that obligation), Jeanne promised. Insincere promises, although imperfect, are still promises. In *Fickle Groom*, Matt does not behave the way that a recently married man should. Although his behavior right after the ceremony is far from ideal, his marrying words at the marriage ceremony still constitute a marriage.

There is plenty of room for people to disagree about which defects are fatal and which ones are not. And this is certainly true of the examples just cited. I'll explore these issues as the book proceeds. In the meantime, though, we already see that there are lots of ways for an utterance to go awry and some defects are more important than others.

§ 2.7   Taking a Deeper Dive on the Nature of Illocution

This section addresses a somewhat technical debate in the philosophy of speech acts, and it might not be of interest to all readers. If one can do without a deep dive into the nature of illocutionary acts, then feel free to skip this section. Understanding the rest of the book will not depend on reading it.

It is fairly common in the philosophy of language to identify two accounts of speech acts: Intentionalism and Conventionalism.[9] Each of these accounts aim to explain exactly how it is that an utterance can be a certain illocutionary act. To make this concrete, consider the following.

> *Promise*: Sarah and Aire are roommates. Sarah is planning a party and Aire needs his sleep. After discussing their mutual expectations, Sarah says to Aire, "I promise to end the party by midnight".

Sarah's utterance is a promise. That is not in dispute. What is a source of contention, by contrast, concerns what exactly makes it a promise. Is it a promise because of Sarah's intention to undertake an obligation to Aire to end the party by midnight? On this Intentionalist way of thinking, Sarah's promissory intention, along perhaps with its recognition, makes it the case that this utterance is a promise. Or, alternatively, is it a promise because Sarah's utterance conforms to a shared social practice of promising? On this Conventionalist line of thinking, individual promises are made possible by that shared social practice. So, just as the rules of American football make a touchdown possible, so too, a shared social practice of promising makes individual promises possible.

Here is one reason to care about this difference; these two camps can give different answers in certain sorts of cases. To see this, consider the following.

> *Party Promise*: Greg is planning a party. Knowing that Greg is extremely anxious that his party will be a flop, his good friend Joe reassures him by saying, "Listen dude, I'll be there; it'll be great. Relax". In saying this, Joe intends to be reassuring Greg; Joe is merely describing his current intention to attend the party; Joe is not intending to promise; that is, he is not intending to undertake an obligation to Greg to attend.

In *Party Promise*, an Intentionalist would say that precisely because Joe did not intend to promise, he did not promise, and this is so even if it is perfectly reasonable for others to think that he did promise. On an Intentionalist picture, the speaker's intentions are paramount. On a Conventionalist understanding of illocution, by contrast, it could well turn out that Joe promised. After all, Joe's utterance accords with the social practice of promising; it is reasonably taken as a promise; it socially counts a promise; others take Joe to have promised and will hold him accountable to that promise. According to Conventionalism, the mere fact that Joe did not intend to promise does not disqualify it as a promise.

It is tempting to think, as many seem to do, that these two frameworks are entirely distinct, are in direct competition, and are constitutive of a difference in kind. After all, if intentions are the basis for illocution, then conventions are not. And, vice versa. If social conventions are the core underpinnings of illocution, then speaker intentions are not.

I reject this polarized picture.

There is considerable overlap between these two "camps". After all, conventions play a crucial role for Intentionalists, and intentions play an integral role for Conventionalists. When Sarah promises Arie, for example, she manages to convey her promissory intention to Aire in large part because of a shared social practice of doing so. Seen in this light, shared social practices are an important part of how it all works for an Intentionalist. The situation is similar with Conventionalism. Sarah's utterance conforms to the shared practice of promising in large part because Sarah intends to promise; having certain complex intentions are a very important part of the very social practices that undergird illocution, at least according to Conventionalism. Given this, one might begin to wonder what the real difference is between these two camps.

Disagreement emerges in extreme cases. Is it possible to promise in the absence of a social practice of doing so? Intentionalists will say Yes. If a speaker can somehow manage to get her promissory intention across to the addressee, then it's a promise even in the absence of a social practice of promising. Tim Scanlon offers the following example in support of this.

> *State of Nature*: Suppose that I am stranded in a strange land. In an attempt to get myself something to eat, I make a spear. I am not very good at using it, however, and when I hurl it at a deer, it goes wide of the mark and sails across a narrow but fast running river. As I stand there gazing forlornly at my spear, lodged on the opposite back, a boomerang comes sailing across and lands near me. Soon a strange person appears on the opposite bank, picks up my spear, and looks around in a puzzled way, evidently searching for the boomerang. It now occurs to me that I might regain my spear without getting wet by getting this person to believe that if he throws my spear across the river I will return his boomerang.

Suppose that I am successful in this: I get him to form the belief; he returns the spear; and I walk off into the woods with it, leaving the boomerang where it fell.[10]

Scanlon argues that this scenario involves a promise. This is because the spear is returned only because of a shared understanding that the boomerang will be returned too. Scanlon argues that this is a broken promise (and it is thus wrong and blameworthy in all the same ways). Since there is no possibility of any shared social practice of promising between the two hunters who come from two distinct cultures that have had no prior contact with one another, this example demonstrates, at least according to Scanlon, that individual acts of promising are possible in the absence of a promising practice. Promises, Scanlon contends, depend only on the communication of an intention to promise. There is, of course, room to disagree.[11]

A Conventionalist will deny that this is a possibility. According to the Conventionalist, whatever such a speaker manages to do with her words, it will, in the absence of a shared social practice of promising, fall short of a full-fledged promise. According to Conventionalism, promises depend, for the very possibility of their existence, on an antecedent social practice performing. To see more clearly what the Conventionalist is thinking here, consider a checkmate in chess. The checkmate move is made possible by the rules of chess. Without those rules, there could be no such thing as a checkmate. Suppose that on a far-off planet of aliens, an artist creates what looks like a chess board; even if an alien moves one of those pieces just so, it won't be a checkmate in a culture that does not include the game of chess.

Another source of disagreement was evident above in *Party Promise*. It concerns whether a speaker can unintentionally perform an illocution. As we saw, Conventionalists will say Yes. If an utterance conforms to a shared social practice of promising, then it is a promise and this is so even if Joe did not intend to promise.

Intending to promise will typically be a part of promising but it is not absolutely required, at least according to Conventionalists. Intentionalists, by contrast, will deny that such an utterance is a promise. It might be mistaken for a promise and it might even socially count as a promise, but if Joe did not intend to undertake the promissory obligation, then it was not a real promise. That's the story, at least according to Intentionalism.

Despite these differences, there is a lot of overlap between these two "camps". This is because, in the vast majority cases, Intentionalists and Conventionalists will agree on the speech act being performed. After all, we typically intend to be performing the very speech action that our utterance socially counts as being.

In light of all this overlap, I prefer to think about this dispute—not as a difference in kind (as it often portrayed)—but as a difference of emphasis and in what is treated as explanatorily primary.[12] For Intentionalists, conventions and social practices play a crucial role but their explanations of illocution will bottom out in terms of speaker intentions. Essentially, Sarah's utterance is a promise because Sarah intended to promise. And, Joe's utterance is *not* a promise because he did not intend to promise. At least, this is the bottom line for an Intentionalist.

For Conventionalism, by contrast, intentions play an important role, but their explanations of illocution will bottom out in terms of conventions and shared social practices. For the Conventionalist, at bottom, Sarah's utterance is a promise because of our shared social practice of promising and because Sarah's utterance conforms to that set of practices. The same goes for Joe's utterance. If there were no such practices, neither Sarah's utterance nor Joe's could have been a promise, at least according to Conventionalism.

If this is really a difference in emphasis (and in what is treated as explanatorily primary), then we should probably stop talking about Intentionalism and Conventionalism as if they are two distinct and opposed positions. Instead, we should acknowledge a range of possible positions, with what we might call Pure Intentionalism at one end of the spectrum and Pure Conventionalism at the other end. Positions in the middle will treat intentions and social practices as playing an equally important constitutive role in illocution.

Even this continuum picture is an oversimplification both of the conceptual space and of the truth about speech acts. This is because other things, besides intentions and conventions, can—and do—play an essential role in fixing facts about illocution. Things like social norms, social relations, shared understanding, conceptual and representational resources (just to name a few) also play an integral role in an utterance constituting whatever illocutionary acts it constitutes. In light of this then, we should envision additional axes for each of these additional factors. Then, there are various positions along a continuum on each axis according to how primary that thing is taken to be in constituting illocution. Now, we move from a spectrum of positions between Pure Intentionalism at one end and Pure Conventionalism at the other to a multi-dimensional space of possible positions.

Here is a further complication. There is no reason why we have to treat all speech acts the same.[13] It could very well be, for example, that different sorts of illocutions belong in different places in our multi-dimensional space; this is because different sorts of things make different sorts of illocutions possible. To see this, consider one of Austin's favorite examples, that of officially naming a ship. This is a formal, highly institutionalized, and proceduralized speech act. Pure Conventionalism makes good sense here. That Pure Conventionalism is a respectable account of this speech act is no reason to think that it is the right account for all speech acts. Consider, for example, sexual consent. Arguably, it is quite troubling if Conventionalism generates the result that a person could unintentionally consent to sex; that socially counting as consenting is constitutive of consenting. Here, Pure Intentionalism makes good sense. Given the morally transformative character of consent, one might be highly reluctant to divorce the illocution from speaker intention.

Here is another complication. It could even be that individual instances of a single type of speech act belong in different places in our multi-dimensional space. It could well be, for instance, that asserting in a court of law is more convention-dependent than asserting in other contexts. And, it could well be that consenting to sex is more intention-dependent than consenting to a contract or to the sale of one's car.[14]

Speech acts are complex, multifarious, and messy; it should be no surprise then the same is true of theories accounting for them. This completes our deep dive. It's time to come back up to the surface and move on to think about how to define silencing. That's the topic of the next chapter.

3

What Is Silencing Anyway?

The purpose of this chapter is to clarify the nature of silencing while also leaving room for disagreement. I will proceed in stages. The first step is to think about definitions. Since how we define silencing will affect the entire investigation, it makes sense for us to first give some thought to the project of defining things. That's the focus of § 3.1. Then, in § 3.2, I will offer a partial definition of silencing; this partial definition will identify an important—and indeed necessary—condition of silencing; it will also explicitly identify what is being left open. The focus for § 3.3 is the identification of three broad categories of silencing. Exploring each one of these three categories shall be the focus of Chapters 4–6, respectively.

§ 3.1 On Definitions

It might seem that defining a word is really simple; all you have to do is look it up in the dictionary. If only it were that easy. It isn't.

The way philosophers have traditionally understood definitions involves identifying necessary and sufficient conditions. So, on this view of definitions, a definition of the term 'water' would identify the conditions that are necessary for something to be water along with the conditions that are sufficient for something to be water. No problem, right? Water is H_2O. Science says so.

Ok, well what about impurities in water? When are there enough impurities to make it a mixture other than water? Is ice water? Is steam? These questions arise about what is required for something to be H_2O but other cases that are a problem for this definition do

On Silencing. Mary Kate McGowan, Oxford University Press. © Mary Kate McGowan 2026.
DOI: 10.1093/9780197837320.003.0003

not hinge on any unclarities about what is H_2O. To see this, suppose that we discover a planet just like Earth in every respect except that the stuff that H_2O does here has a different chemical composition. Putnam, the philosopher who came up with this thought experiment, called that substance XYZ.[1] On this Twin Earth, XYZ falls from the sky when it rains and fills the disposable water bottles at the gym. XYZ does on Twin Earth everything that H_2O does on earth. So, is XYZ water? In discovering XYZ, have we discovered a new kind of water or is XYZ disqualified since it is not H_2O? If we actually have a true definition of water, that definition would identify all necessary and sufficient conditions for the correct application of the term 'water,' so it would absolutely settle all questions about how to apply the term. Putnam used this case to show (among other things) that we do not really have true definitions for our terms, and this is so even in well-established scientific cases.

What now? If true definitions are elusive, then I cannot hope to actually define silencing. That's true but all is not lost. I can offer a partial definition. And, I will do so by identifying one necessary condition. I will also be as explicit as possible about the assumptions I am making in constructing that partial definition.

One more thing before I get started. The right way to (partially) define something depends on the purpose that that (partial) definition will serve. The right way to define pornography when explaining to my children what they are not permitted to see is quite different from the right way to define it for some specific legal purpose. In fact, it would be a mistake to think that one and the same (partial) definition ought to serve these very different purposes.

The same is true for a (partial) definition of silencing. Theorists can take an interest in silencing for different reasons, and the right way to characterize silencing can—and indeed should—depend on those reasons. Suppose, for example, that Caroline is interested in exploring how silencing might violate the right to free speech; she's interested in regulating the speech that silences other speech. In that case, the relevant definition of silencing should include only those cases of silencing that are relevant to the free speech right and that are harmful in ways that the law recognizes. Suppose instead that Rob is interested in how silencing undermines the social process of knowledge acquisition. Rob's concern is that when people are silenced, their knowledge is not being properly incorporated into what counts as socially shared knowledge. The right way to define silencing for Rob's purposes will be different (and probably much broader) than for Caroline's purposes.

In the next section, I turn to the task of identifying a reasonable partial definition of silencing. That partial definition should get at the core of silencing but also be compatible with a variety of different theoretical purposes. For this reason, I shall pack less into the definition, rather than more.[2] Leaving it open for others to add conditions to their definition of silencing thus allowing their more specific definition to suit their particular theoretical purposes.

§ 3.2 On Silencing

My primary aim in partially defining silencing is to capture a theoretically useful characterization of it that gets at the core phenomenon without excluding more specific characterizations that are suitable for narrower theoretical purposes. To this end, this partial definition should do several things. It should identify a phenomenon that is important and worthy of our concern and of our collective attempts to understand it. It should also be something that is definitely related to speech and communication. After all, silencing is a distinctly speech-related issue. Finally, an adequate characterization should help to make sense of the sorts of cases discussed at the beginning of this book. It should explain why they are (or are not) silencing.

Again, I will strive to avoid building controversial assumptions into the definition. And, I think that this is the right thing to do when there are different theoretical purposes at play and potential sources of disagreement at issue. In the process, I will flag many of those issues.

In working toward a reasonable partial definition of silencing, I will consider various potential necessary conditions. For each of these potential necessary conditions, I will consider whether that condition is strictly necessary for the core phenomenon of silencing and, if not, whether that condition ought to be necessary for some more detailed characterization of silencing (that is, appropriate relative to some theoretical purpose). To make this more concrete, one might decide that being harmful isn't necessary for something to be silencing, and so harmfulness is not a necessary condition of the core concept of silencing. That said, one might nevertheless think that Caroline ought to build harmfulness into her working definition since, relative to her purpose (of identifying something that warrants legal intervention), harmfulness is required.

In what follows, the reader should keep two sources of potential disagreement in mind. The first concerns whether a certain condition should be a necessary condition so that anything failing to meet that condition would automatically fail to be an instance of silencing. A second potential source of disagreement concerns disagreement over how to understand a particular necessary condition. That is, there might be agreement that a certain condition is required for something to be silencing but there is nevertheless disagreement about what is involved in meeting that condition.

§ 3.2.1 A Necessary Condition: Communicative Failure

Our core concept should be distinctly speech-related, account for our interest in it, and square with many or most of the motivating cases. Let's refresh our memories and consider those sorts of cases again.[3]

Soundproof Box: A stressed out and desperate father, Michael, finds himself unable to tolerate the relentless banter of his high-energy three-year old son, Johnny. So, whenever Michael really needs some headspace, he lovingly places little Johnny inside a small but cozy soundproof box that Michael built for this very purpose.

Duct Tape: Joe is robbing Margot; concerned that she might scream and alert her neighbors, Joe places duct tape on her mouth.

Refusing Help: Cindy says, "No, really, thank you but it's important to me to do this myself; I can do it and I would not want to trouble you unnecessarily," in order to politely decline Carl's generous offer of help. Unable to shake his view of women as damsels in distress, Carl interprets Cindy as politely accepting his help.

No Police Report: Linda is a Black woman who experiences domestic abuse. She decides against reporting it to the police because she knows full well that the only result of doing so would be to reinforce the stereotype, already present in the minds of the police, that Black men are violent.[4]

Woman Boss: Jane is the boss but when she orders her employees to do things, they tend to interpret her as issuing suggestions. When they fail to do what she orders, they regard her as unreasonable for expecting them to do it and when they do it, they resent her for not thanking them properly. All in all, they come to see her as a rude and incompetent boss.[5]

Dismissed Witness: Claire is an unhoused person who witnesses a street crime; she testifies at trial but the jury dismisses her testimony. Presumably because she is unhoused, they judge her to be without credibility.

There are different things going on in these various cases. In *Soundproof Box*, for example, Little Johnny is able to speak but, being inside a soundproof box, no one is able to hear him. In *Duct Tape*, by contrast, Margot is physically prevented from saying anything or from making any noise. In *Refusing Help*, Cindy speaks and her words are heard perfectly well, but her polite refusal is mistaken for something else. Linda, in *No Police Report*, doesn't actually say anything; she decides against speaking but decides this because she knows that her audience is affected by stereotypes and her utterance would only serve to reinforce them. In *Woman Boss*, Jane speaks but her order is mistaken for a suggestion and her employees think less of her as a result of their mistakes. Finally, Claire, in *Dismissed Witness* speaks, is heard, and is understood perfectly well; it's just that she is not believed.

Despite the various differences, all of these cases involve something going wrong with speech.[6] Speech is not heard (or seen or read); speech is misunderstood; speech is not believed; speech is prevented altogether. Now, the main purpose of language is to facilitate communication. Arguably, enabling *communication* is what makes speech so valuable.[7]

One way to see this is to consider a legal right to free speech. A legal free speech principle amounts to a legal system making it more difficult to regulate speech. The basic thought is that speech is valuable in ways that warrant extending special protections to it. Several justifications for this practice have been offered, and they each rely essentially on the communicative capacity of speech. One such justification is called the argument from democracy.[8] It maintains that speech must be free in order for a democracy to function as it should. This is because we need to be able to say what we think in order to openly discuss issues of public concern; we need to be able to tell our representatives what we want them to do, and we need to be able to criticize the government. And, doing these things requires *communication*, not just the production of sound, or written symbols, or other signs. We cannot fruitfully discuss issues of public concern without communicating with one another about them. It is not enough to produce meaningful sounds if they are never heard or are not understood properly. On this way of understanding what justifies a free speech right then, speech is valuable because of its crucial role in facilitating communication.

Soundproof Box offers another way to see this. In this case, Johnny is able to produce speech. He can say whatever he wants and he can even be as loud as he wants. Speech production is not hindered in Johnny's case but, because no one can hear him, Johnny is utterly unable to communicate. The whole point of speech, it seems, is to communicate. This suggests that the production of speech in and of itself is not what we value. Rather, what we value is the ability to communicate with one another.

On this way of thinking then, communication is the core function of speech and thus the core issue with silencing. At its heart then, silencing involves something going wrong with communication; call this communicative failure.

Going forward, I treat communicative failure as a necessary condition of silencing. And, doing so squares with the three goals for a reasonable partial definition of silencing. Communicative failure is speech-related; it's clearly worthy of our study, attention, and concern, and it appears to capture what is pertinent about the various motivating cases above. So far, so good. As we shall see, though, what constitutes communicative failure is controversial.

Here is one source of potential disagreement. It concerns a distinction between communicative failure (where a communication fails in some way) and communicative interference (where something gets in the way of a communication and leads to its failure). To get a sense of what this distinction is meant to capture, consider the following two cases:

> *Distracted Husband*: Sam tells his husband, Gareth, that the cable guy is coming between 7 am and 7 pm but Gareth is so distracted by the inner workings of his brilliant mind that Sam's utterance doesn't register at all.

> *Controlling Dictator*: A dictator decides that he does not want an-
> yone who disagrees with his policies to be able to criticize his re-
> gime so he installs complex sound-cancelling devices throughout
> his kingdom; these devices are activated whenever dissidents
> verbally express criticism. This Alexa-like technology reliably
> detects criticism and then generates perturbations of air that
> cancel out the verbalization of that criticism before it impinges
> on anyone's eardrums.[9]

In *Distracted Husband*, there is communicative failure because
Gareth fails to recognize what Sam told him. Although there is
communicative failure here, there does not seem to be any interference; Gareth is merely distracted; nothing external appears to have
gotten in the way of Sam's communication. In *Controlling Dictator*,
by contrast, there is both communicative failure and communicative interference. There is communicative failure because, although
the dissidents are able to say what they want, their criticisms are
not being heard so they are unable to communicate their criticisms
to anyone. There is also interference in *Controlling Dictator* because the Alexa-like criticism-cancelling devices block dissidents'
attempts to communicate. Intuitively then, it seems that communicative interference requires that an obstacle or barrier interferes
with the communication in question and leads to its failure.

It's tempting to think that perhaps communicative interference, and not communicative failure, ought to be required for
silencing.[10] One might think, that is, that the dissidents are silenced
in *Controlling Dictator* but that Sam is not silenced in *Distracted
Husband*. And, this might be because the Alexa-like devices interfere with the dissidents' attempts to communicate but Sam faces no
such obstacle.

Despite this line of thinking, which I grant is intuitive, I am
not inclined to treat communicative interference as required for
silencing. There are two reasons for this. This is because this notion of interference is insufficiently clear to do the required work.

In short, it either requires more elaboration or it falls apart. To see this, notice that if there is communicative failure, *something* must have caused that failure, and maybe we should then say that that thing interfered. In other words, perhaps Gareth's overactive mind interfered with Sam's communication so *Distracted Husband* involves communicative interference after all. If one does not want to say that all cases of communicative failure are cases of communicative interference, then one must be prepared to say more about what makes something a case of interference. Must it be something external or something out of the ordinary? There is work to be done here. And, unless and until that work is satisfactorily done, I for one will refrain from relying on this insufficiently defined notion of interference.

For this reason, I henceforth focus on communicative failure, and I think I can be sufficiently clear about what it entails.

That's true but it requires being clear about how narrowly or broadly we understand communication. And, this issue is something theorists can disagree about. To get a sense of this source of controversy, consider a revised version of the *Controlling Dictator* case:

> *Controlling Dictator: Sincerity Version*: A dictator installs devices throughout his kingdom that cause hearers to believe that dissidents are liars, and their sincere regime-criticizing assertions are lies.

Would being caused to mistake sincere claims for insincere ones be a form of communicative failure? Some might well say No. After all, the claims are successfully communicated since hearers recognize both that and what the dissidents are asserting. Consequently, there is an important sense in which the *communication* of that claim does *not* fail. Others might well say Yes. After all, these regime-criticizing claims won't have the impact they ought to have, and this is exactly because they are mistaken for lies. Barriers to appropriate impact after successful communication takes place might reasonably be treated as a form of communicative failure. After all, if the whole point of communicating is to make these sorts of changes in the world, then it seems that we ought to include their prevention as a kind of failure.

To add some weight to this broader way of thinking about communication and hence what counts as its failure, consider another case.

> *Not Even Minimal Consideration*: A dictator installs chips into the brains of each of his citizens that prevent any criticism of his regime from affecting the hearer's beliefs in any way whatsoever.[11]

In this case, the citizens are able to hear and understand the criticisms but all criticism is prevented from having any impact at all on anyone's beliefs. So, dissidents in *Not Even Minimal Consideration* are free to criticize the government, and they are even able to successfully communicate their criticisms, it's just that these criticisms are prevented from having any impact at all. A consideration of this kind of case suggests that we care about more than just communication in the strict sense; we also care about its impact, at least minimally.

Duct Tape affords yet another consideration in favor of expanding our understanding of communicative failure even further. In *Duct Tape*, Margot is prevented from making any verbal sounds and thus from attempting to communicate with speech at all. Because of this, neither of the above conceptions of communicative failure are apt. Since she did not even attempt to say anything, there were no recognition failures; no verbal communication was attempted, so no communicative intentions were formed. Moreover, it makes no sense to talk about impact prevention of a communication attempt that never even takes place. For this reason, we need to consider attempt prevention as another potential form of communicative failure.

Going forward, it will be useful to distinguish between *three* different conceptions of communicative failure. They are:

Communicative Failure: Strict Version: Communicative failure involves an addressee not properly recognizing some aspect of what a speaker is trying to communicate.

Communicative Failure: Impact Version: Communicative failure (also) involves the prevention of the impact that a communication ought to have.[12]

Communicative Failure: Prevention Version: Communicative failure (also) involves the prevention of a particular communication attempt.

As *Controlling Dictator: Sincerity Version* demonstrates, these conceptions of communicative failure differ. This case satisfies the impact version of communicative failure (because the dissidents are not believed) but not the strict version (because the claims are communicated). These three conceptions of communicative failure will be useful in the exploration that follows.

In sum then, communicative failure is necessary for silencing but there is some disagreement about how exactly and how broadly to understand such failure.

§ 3.2.2 Other Potential Necessary Conditions

I now consider other potential necessary conditions of silencing. Although I will argue against them as necessary conditions for our reasonable partial definition of silencing, each of them tracks something worthy of our attention. In other words, these conditions might identify a subclass of silencing especially worthy of attention and they each might be an appropriate necessary condition for a more detailed definition of silencing (that is suitable for a more specific theoretical purpose).

One such potential condition is called *systematicity*. To motivate it, consider the following case.

> *Noisy Truck*: Gary criticizes his pastor just as a big noisy truck passes by and drowns out what he says so that no one else actually hears him.

Noisy Truck is a candidate instance of silencing because it involves communicative failure, our one necessary condition. In point of fact, *Noisy Truck* satisfies both the strict and the impact version of communicative failure. It satisfies the strict version since the pastor does not hear what Gary says so Gary does not manage to communicate his criticism to the pastor. *Noisy Truck* also satisfies the impact version, since Gary's criticism will not have its intended impact since no one actually heard what he said. Despite these results, one might nevertheless think that *Noisy Truck* should not count as silencing. After all, what happens here is haphazard, one-off, and idiosyncratic. On this line of thinking, only instances of communicative failure that are systematically brought about, as in say *Controlling Dictator*, should count as silencing. These sorts of considerations support treating systematicity as a further necessary condition of silencing.

Elsewhere, I have included systematicity as a necessary condition of silencing (and so do several others). I do so because I am interested in oppression and the possibility that silencing is a component of it. Given the structural nature of oppression, one-off instances of communicative failure would not count. For this reason, I build systematicity in. In general, any theorist interested in silencing as a structural phenomenon would do well to treat systematicity as necessary. Notice how the motivation for building systematicity into the definition is driven by a theoretical interest in structural harms. Relative to *that* aim, systematicity ought to be required.

Despite these considerations and despite what I have said else-where, I will not *here* treat systematicity as necessary for silencing. There are several reasons for this. First, there are reasons to regard Gary as silenced in *Noisy Truck* even if we are less concerned about such haphazard instances. After all, Gary does not manage to get his criticism across; the truck prevents his speech from doing what he aims to do and what is valuable about speech. Second, I do not want to assume that everyone interested in silencing is interested in it as a structural issue. In short, I want to leave room for less specific definitions of silencing that are appropriate for other purposes. Third, this systematicity condition is not fully defined in the liter-ature and it remains unclear how it ought to be defined. That said, several theorists have offered partial characterizations.[13]

Although I am not building systematicity into the partial defi-nition, systematicity nevertheless ought to remain on our col-lective radar screens. Arguably, it is an important feature of any case involving it and its presence justifies additional interest and concern.

Another potential necessary condition of silencing is *harmful-ness*. To highlight the controversy over this potential necessary condition, consider the following case:

No Harm, No Foul: Jonah says, "Lovely dogwoods" to a passerby while he is walking along a riverbank but, unknown to him, the random passerby is so enthralled with the beautiful surround-ings that Jonah's utterance goes unprocessed.

Jonah experiences communicative failure; the passerby does not properly receive his intended message. As a result, this is a candi-date instance of silencing. That said, one might nevertheless doubt that Jonah is really silenced here. After all, it makes no difference to Jonah's life whether or not this random stranger catches his pleasantries during this nature walk. There might be communica-tive failure but it seems utterly unimportant, even trivial. In light of this, one might regard the harmlessness of what happens to Jonah here as a reason to deny that this is an instance of silencing. To do so would be to treat harmfulness as a necessary condition of silencing.

Although there are such reasons to treat harmfulness as necessary, I will not.[14] Again, this is so I do not foreclose any possibilities at the outset and I leave room for alternative definitions suited to alternative theoretical purposes. That said, there are further reasons to avoid treating harmfulness as necessary; doing so would require quite a lot of additional theoretical work. The nature of harm, which particular harms are associated with silencing, and how to establish that such harms actually obtain are each quite complex and controversial.

Of course, denying that harmfulness ought to be a necessary condition for the partial definition of silencing is perfectly compatible with harmfulness being an otherwise important aspect of a case. First, harmfulness warrants special concern, and second, it might well be an appropriate necessary condition for a more detailed definition. Anyone interested in potential legal intervention, for example, would need to focus on cases that involve legally recognized harms.

I shall now consider one last potential necessary condition of silencing. One might regard silencing as a *group-based* phenomenon. Going this route means that it is only silencing when the communicative failure obtains because the (silenced) person is a member of a certain social group. So, the only cases of communicative failure that count as silencing, on this view, would be cases brought about by the silenced person's social identity. Let's try to get a sense of how this might work.

Suppose that Janet's assertion that it will rain tomorrow is completely misunderstood by Sadie because Sadie holds a peculiar belief that almost no one else holds, namely that anyone who has floppy earlobes (as Janet does) says the exact opposite of what they mean. Under these circumstances, Janet's assertion that it will rain tomorrow fails to be communicated to Sadie because Sadie takes

Jane to be communicating that it will *not* rain tomorrow. Although Jane here experiences communicative failure (in the strict sense), that this happens has nothing whatsoever to do with Sadie's social identity.[15] After all, those who have floppy earlobes do not constitute any kind of social group. If, however, Sadie were to misunderstand Janet's assertion because Sadie believes that all Muslims or all women are ironic in this way, then this case of communicative failure would be group-based, and thus it would be eligible to be silencing on this group-based account.

I will not be treating group-basedness as a necessary condition of silencing either and the reasons are by now familiar. First, I want to leave open the possibility that people can be silenced for other sorts of reasons. Holding an unpopular opinion, for example, can interfere with the successful communication of one's views but the holding of that unpopular opinion need not constitute a social identity. Furthermore, we are all familiar with cases where communication breaks down between people holding different political commitments and, again, in most contexts anyway, the holding of such commitments does not mark out a social group. Since I want the partial definition of silencing to be open to these important possibilities, I will not treat group-basedness as necessary. Another reason to avoid building it in is that theorists can and do disagree about the nature of group-basedness and which groups (ought to) count. And, it is best to avoid such controversies where I can.

Despite the fact that I am not here requiring that silencing happen in virtue of a person's social group membership, one might well want to pay special attention to cases of communicative failure that are group-based in this way. If one has a theoretical interest in tracking the various ways that members of certain social groups are socially disadvantaged, for example, cases of group-based silencing certainly ought to count. Moreover, anyone with that particular theoretical interest should build being group-based in as a necessary condition of their definition of silencing.

In sum, I have argued against treating systematicity, harmfulness, or being group-based as necessary conditions of silencing. That said, it nevertheless makes good sense to build them into other definitions (depending on the theoretical aim of those definitions). Even though these conditions are not treated as necessary for current purposes, there is nevertheless good reason to believe that we ought to be especially concerned about cases of silencing that do involve them. Thus, even though I am not building these features into my definition of silencing, central cases of silencing may well have these features.

I am, by contrast, treating communicative failure as necessary. As we have already seen, doing so squares with our three aims in identifying a reasonable partial definition. Communicative failure is a distinctly speech-related issue; it is worthy of our attention and concern, and it makes good sense of the various motivating cases with which we started. Although communicative failure is required for silencing, there is nevertheless disagreement about what constitutes such failure, and this will make a difference in what follows.

§ 3.3 The Three Broad Categories of Silencing

As mentioned in Chapter 1, it is helpful to distinguish between three broad categories of silencing: cases where a communication is attempted but it fails in some way, cases where something prevents a potential communication from even being attempted, and cases where the proper impact of a communication is prevented.[16]

In the first type, silencing occurs during a communication attempt. In the second type, silencing prevents a communication attempt and thus precedes it.[17] And, in the third type, the silencing happens after the communication attempt; in particular, the silencing prevents that communication from having its proper impact.[18]

There will be a lot more to say about each of these categories but, in what follows, we consider a few examples just to give each of them a little concreteness.

The first type involves communicative failure with an attempted communication.[19] In *Refusing Help*, for example, something goes wrong with Cindy's speech act; in particular, Carl fails to realize that Cindy is refusing his offer; consequently, Cindy fails to communicate her refusal to Carl. In this case, it seems that Carl's view of women as damsels in distress interferes with Cindy's ability to communicate her refusal to him. Mishearing what someone says or what someone means by what they say would be additional examples of this broad type of silencing.

The second category involves preventing a communication attempt altogether. This can happen in many ways. Consider, for instance, a person who is gagged and thereby physically prevented from speaking. Or, someone who is ordered to remain silent. Other cases of this, however, will involve decisions against speaking. To see an example of this, consider poor Michael in *Sound-Proof Box*. Suppose that Michael comes to realize that no one will hear him while he is in the box so he decides to save his energy and keep quiet. In this case, Michael's awareness of the futility of speaking causes him to decide against it; it just isn't worth his effort. This version of the case can be understood as an example of communication attempt prevention. So can *No Police Report*. These cases both involve decisions against speaking in anticipation of something going wrong if one were to speak.

The third broad type involves prevention of the impact of a communication. Assertions that are illegitimately dismissed, orders that should be but are not followed, and refusals that are not respected are all examples of impact prevention and thus fall into this third category. *Dismissed Witness* is a case in point. Of course, we cannot expect every speech act to have the impact the speaker wants or hopes for, so more work will need to be done in identifying the appropriate impact of a communication and thus which types of impact prevention matter for our purposes.[20]

Marking these distinctions is useful but it is also important to notice that these various types of silencing can interact with one another. If something interferes with an attempted communication, for example, this will in all likelihood undermine the impact of that communication. If a speaker anticipates that her attempted communication will be misunderstood, she might well decide against speaking. There are lots of possibilities of interactions between various types (and sub-types) of silencing, and I shall explore them in what follows.

§ 3.4 Revisiting Sincerity and Communication

I'd like to revisit, and further complicate, an issue we addressed above (in § 3.2.1), concerning whether speaker sincerity is communicated in the narrow sense. In that section, it was suggested that failure to recognize a speaker's sincerity can constitute impact but not strict communicative failure. Let's now look a bit more closely at this issue. As we shall now see, it's complicated. As a matter of fact, it depends. Sometimes, a speaker *is* intending to communicate their own sincerity and, when they are, a failure to recognize it can be strict communicative failure. To investigate this issue more clearly, we should briefly revisit the complex meta-intentional nature of communicative intentions.

Recall from Chapter 2 that communication is meta-intentional. To see this, we will first consider a case where that meta-intention is missing. Suppose that John wants Bill to believe that John is wealthy so John says things indicating a familiarity with the upper east side of Manhattan and with Newport's Bailey's Beach. Although John intends for Bill to believe that John is rich, John does *not* intend for Bill to believe this *via* Bill's recognition of John's intention to cause Bill to believe this. So, even if John succeeds in causing Bill to believe that John is rich, this is not a case of communication. And, it's not a case of communication precisely because John lacks the required meta-intention.

Contrast that with a different case. Suppose now that John is trying to convince Bill to go into business with him and Bill has just expressed concern that they lack the required capital to be successful. When John hands Bill a copy of an email from his financial advisor indicating that his net worth exceeds 113 million US $, John both intends to cause Bill to believe that he is rich and he intends to do so via Bill's recognition of that very intention. This is what it means for communication to be meta-intentional.[21] John intends to cause this belief *and* he intends for that intention to be recognized by Bill.

At first blush anyway, it seems that the sincerity of a speech act is *not* part of its communicative content[22]; and this is because the required meta-intention seems to be missing. To see this, consider an ordinary assertion. When a speaker asserts something, the speaker typically intends for the addressee to believe that the speaker is sincere but the speaker does *not* intend for the addressee to believe this *via* the addressee's recognition of that intention. In other words, the speaker isn't *telling* the addressee that they are sincere; they just are and they want that recognized. If this is correct, then whenever a sincere utterance is mistaken for an insincere one, it is not communicative failure in the strict sense. Just as we suggested above, it could (only) be—or cause—communicative impact failure. Assertions, that are taken to be insincere, won't be believed, so their impact will be prevented but the assertion itself is successfully communicated despite the failure to recognize its sincerity.

If all speech acts work the same way, we could rest content with the above assessment.[23] As it stands, however, speech acts vary in a myriad of ways and the (communicative) role of sincerity is one of them. To see this, consider the following case.

Adamant Parent: In the recent past, Jay has been too flexible with his son's bedtime. Determined to set—and to enforce—better boundaries, Jay says, with a stern look and a penetrating glare, "Bedtime is 8:00 sharp. [pause] Not. [pause] Negotiable."

Now, we already know that what a speaker means goes well beyond what a speaker explicitly says, so might Jay's sincerity actually be part of what Jay intends to communicate here? I think it sure can. In *Adamant Parent*, Jay is communicating the content of what he says but he is also communicating his sincerity in saying it. In particular, Jay means to get across something like 'and I mean it this time'. Jay both intends to cause his son to believe that he means it this time *and* he intends to cause this belief *via* his son's recognition of that very intention. In *Adamant Parent* then, Jay is essentially telling his son that he is sincere; Jay speaker means his own sincerity.[24]

Come to think of it, this sincerity-communicating phenomenon does not just apply to assertions; plenty of other sorts of speech actions can involve the communication of sincerity too. To see this, consider the following examples.

Generous Offer: Gwen owns an extra car and wants to offer its use to her new neighbor. Aware that this offer is unusually generous, Gwen wants to emphasize that she means it sincerely when she says "Honestly, it's no trouble at all. In fact, I'll feel better if the car is getting some use."

Emphatic Denial: Nellie has been accused of stealing a cupcake from the communal refrigerator in the employee lounge. Having been a jokester in the past, Nellie is concerned that she is under real suspicion, so she stresses that she means it when she says "I didn't do it; Really! I'll even swear on my dead cat's grave!"

Reassuring Promise: Lisa and Mary are really good friends. Lisa is extremely anxious about going to their high school reunion because she knows that she will see her (spectacularly awful) ex-husband there. Mary promises to go with her to the reunion.

Given the high stakes, Mary stresses that she intends to keep her promise to Lisa when she says, "I swear I will be by your side. There is no way I am letting my best friend deal with the sight of that sack of rancid fecal matter without a supportive friend. You can count on me. 100%."

In each of these cases, speakers are intending to communicate their own sincerity. And, if the addressee were to fail to recognize the speaker's sincerity in any of these cases, then we would have communicative failure in the strict sense. So, despite what was suggested in § 3.2.1, failure to recognize speaker sincerity can be strict communication failure. So, whether sincere speech acts that are mistaken for insincere ones are candidate cases of strict communicative failure will depend on whether the speaker speaker-means their own sincerity. Since this varies from case to case and context to context, I cannot offer the same diagnosis in every instance. Given the complexity of speech actions, this should not be a surprise. In some contexts, the sincerity of a speech act really matters, participants know this, and speakers intend to communicate their own sincerity. In any particular case, one will just have to look more closely to determine precisely what is within the scope of the speaker's communicative intentions.

§ 3.5 Conclusion

In sum, I have here identified a partial definition of silencing that treats communicative failure as a necessary condition. I considered, and rejected (for my current purposes anyway), several other conditions (e.g., systematicity, harmfulness, and being group-based) as necessary for silencing. Although these conditions are not necessary, they do track features of a case that might warrant additional attention and concern. For this reason, they will come up again as I explore various examples throughout the book.

In the next chapter, I look more closely at cases where something goes wrong with an attempted communication. As we shall see there, there are many ways that things can go awry with an attempted communication and so there are many different mishaps that can be this kind of silencing. An understanding of the complexity of communicative acts will help to highlight the many ways that such acts can be thwarted.

4

You Got That Wrong

On Varieties of Miscommunication

This chapter will explore cases where something goes wrong with a communication attempt. As we saw in Chapter 2, acts of communication are fairly complex actions and they can go wrong in a variety of ways. Because of this, there are many different kinds of communicative mishaps that can count as this broad kind of silencing.

In what follows, I shall start each section with a real-life example; this will require spelling out the relevant context. Then, I will analyze what goes wrong with the attempted communication and then consider whether it's silencing. Additional lessons will be gleaned along the way. After exploring four real-life examples (and what goes wrong in them), I will end the chapter with a survey of these and other ways that communicative attempts can go awry. Doing so will provide us with a menu of communicative mishaps, their differences, and their impact. The more one knows about how communication attempts can be thwarted, the better equipped one is to avoid them, identify them when they happen, and remedy them.

§ 4.1 Example 1: Messing Up Meaning

As we have been stressing, language use does many things and one of the things it does is communicate meaning. So, one of the ways that an attempted communication can go wrong concerns the content or meaning. There are a few different sorts of options here but before I get into that, let's look at an example.

On Silencing. Mary Kate McGowan, Oxford University Press. © Mary Kate McGcwan 2026.
DOI: 10.1093/9780197837320.003.0004

§ 4.1.1 The Case of Prickly Politics: *Yard Sign*

In this section, we are going to consider a concrete example of a communication attempt that goes wrong in some important way. The example we will explore involves two people in the United States who have quite different political orientations. One is a liberal, and the other is a conservative. There are, of course, many different ways to be liberal and many different ways to be conservative. When relevant, further details are presented.

The case is called *Yard Sign*. It is based on a real case (but the names and some of the details have been changed). Here is the case. Bill and Rose are neighbors; Bill is politically liberal, tending to vote Democrat, and Rose is politically conservative, having voted for Republican candidates in the recent past. While getting mail out of their street-side mailboxes, the following exchange takes place between them:

BILL: Look, [gesturing towards a yard sign lying face-down on his front lawn] someone toppled my 'Black Lives Matter' sign. What the hell is wrong with people?

ROSE: [looking over at the yard sign on Bill's lawn, Rose shrugs, and says cheerfully] Looks better that way if you ask me, Bill.

BILL: [Bill stares at Rose, with his mouth agape and his face expressing incredulity and horror]

ROSE: [shaking her head gently in exasperation and with a wry smile while walking back towards her house, Rose says calmly] Have a nice afternoon, Bill.

Here, Bill is genuinely and even visibly horrified by what Rose says to him (that is, 'Looks better that way if you ask me, Bill.') but this is because of what Bill takes Rose to mean by saying it. He takes her to be unapologetically rejecting the sentiment behind his sign; he also takes her to be denying that police brutality against Black people is a systemic problem in the United States. Now, in interpreting her this way, Bill sincerely believes that he has been fairly charitable. After all, he knows her well enough to know that she would definitely not approve of police brutality in any form; he figures instead that she is misinformed about the facts. That she is misinformed, though, really bothers him because, when it comes to an issue as important as this one, Bill fervently believes that a person really ought to take care to get things right and Rose evidently hasn't done this. Bill is therefore sincerely appalled by what he has just learned about his neighbor, Rose.

Despite Bill's interpretive efforts, he is (completely) mistaken about what Rose meant by what she said. Rose does not reject the sentiment behind Bill's yard sign, and she is not misinformed about race and police brutality in the United States. Bill got it entirely wrong. Instead, when Rose said what she said (that is, 'Looks better that way if you ask me, Bill.') Rose intended to be communicating to Bill her disapproval of certain aspects of the Black Lives Matter social movement. In particular, Rose regards all of these BLM yard signs popping up all over rich suburban white neighborhoods as a lazy, ineffectual, and potentially hypocritical form of activism. Since Rose also knows that Bill hasn't actually done anything tangible to make things better for people of color, his sign irritates her more than most and she was happy to see it face down. When Rose said what she said, she fully expected Bill to understand what she meant. She assumed (in this case falsely) that he would be aware of these sorts of concerns about the BLM movement. Furthermore, since Bill knows that Rose volunteers four days a week at a woman's shelter that serves a nearby poor Black community, he also knows (or at least he ought to know) that she favors real action for social justice as opposed to mere signaling about it. When Bill reacted with his look of horror, Rose realized that Bill had somehow misunderstood her. Although Rose did not know exactly what Bill took her to be saying, she decided to leave it alone.

§ 4.1.2 Analyzing What Goes Wrong: Speaker Meaning

Yard Sign involves a fairly straightforward case of miscommunication where the hearer, Bill, misunderstands what the speaker, Rose, means. Bill correctly recognizes the words Rose utters and what those words literally mean, but Bill misidentifies the message that Rose actually intends to convey to him by uttering those words to him in that context.

Recall, from Chapter 2, that when we use language to communicate, what we actually say is typically quite different from what we are primarily trying to get across; what we literally say enables our addressee to figure out what we really mean. Let's revisit an example of this in action:

> *Statin Implicature*: Piotra and Newt are talking about how confused and forgetful their father has been lately, when Piotra says, "Lots of statin medications have neurological side effects".

In *Statin Implicature*, what Piotra actually says is different from what she means to communicate to Newt. Here, Piotra is telling Newt that their father's forgetfulness is caused by his medication but what she actually says (that is, 'Lots of statin medications have neurological side effects') is different from that; it is a general claim about statin drugs and not about their father at all. Piotra successfully communicates her intended message to Newt though because Newt works out what Piotra means by what she says. In this case, Newt correctly identifies Piotra's speaker meaning.

In *Yard Sign,* by contrast, that doesn't happen. Although Bill realizes that Rose means something in addition to what she literally says, he misidentifies what she actually means.[1] Because Bill fails to recognize Rose's intended (speaker) meaning, Rose's communication attempt (in saying 'Looks better that way if you ask me, Bill.') fails; Rose does not in fact get her intended message across.

§ 4.1.3 Is This Silencing?

As we know, silencing requires communicative failure so we now need to decide whether this case involves such failure. Clearly, it does. Exactly because Bill misidentifies Rose's intended message, her attempt to communicate that message to him here fails.

We might wonder why this happened; that is, we might wonder what caused the communicative failure here. Here's one way of thinking about the case. The way I have described the case, it looks like certain facts about Bill's mental state get in the way of Rose's attempted communication. In particular, Bill's beliefs about conservatives coupled with his lack of awareness about some of the criticisms of the BLM movement play a key role in his interpretive mistake. Thinking about it this way, Bill's beliefs interfere with his recognition of Rose's intended meaning and thus prevent her from successfully communicating it to Bill.

Now, it might seem strange to think of Bill's beliefs as running interference in this way. You might think that things like loud speakers and gags can interfere with a person's ability to communicate but another person's beliefs cannot. Although it might seem counterintuitive at first, it makes sense when you stop to think about it, especially in light of the highly inferential nature of communication. When Rose said what she said, she counted on Bill being able to figure out what she meant. She took some background information to be shared between them but that information was not shared, and the fact that it was not shared is what prevented her communication from being successful.

There are two concepts in the philosophy of language that are helpful here. The first is Jennifer Hornsby's notion of reciprocity.[2] Reciprocity is a general condition in an audience such that the audience members' mental states (their beliefs, attitudes, etc.) enable/dispose them to properly understand a speaker. If Monique is speaking French but no one in her audience understands French, for example, then reciprocity fails; Monique will be unable to successfully communicate with her audience because the audience is not equipped to understand her. Similarly, if everyone believes that all well-bred women never refuse a sincere offer of help from a well-bred man, then a woman's refusal of help might well go unrecognized. Her audience is not properly disposed to recognize her intentions and she is communicatively disabled by that.

The second helpful concept, developed by Robert Stalnaker, is common ground; it's specific to particular conversations.[3] It's (basically) the information shared between participants. In order for information to be shared, it's not enough that it's known to each participant. Everyone must also know that everyone else accepts the information. Now, we routinely rely on common ground to effectively communicate. To see this, consider again *Statin Medication*. When Piotra says, "Lots of statin medications have neurological side effects," she successfully communicates to Newt that their father's forgetfulness is being caused by his medication. In doing so, Piotra relies on shared information; in particular, she relies on him knowing (and him knowing that she knows) that their father is currently taking a statin medication. This information being shared is crucial to the success of Piotra's communication.

The way I have set up the case, it sounds like it's Bill's fault; he mistakenly believes that all political conservatives are MAGA conservatives and that's false. Rose is a case in point. We could tweak the case, so Rose bears more responsibility. After all, she certainly could have done more to signal to Bill that her political views are not identical to the narratives being spun by conservative media outlets. While it is certainly true that hearers ought to be charitable when interpreting speakers, it is also true that speakers have communicative responsibilities too. Speakers should take care to give hearers all the clues they need to identify speaker meaning. And, in this case, Rose could have done a better job.

Setting aside issues of communicative responsibility, what goes wrong in *Yard Sign* is essentially a mutually unrecognized lack of shared common ground. This is what leads to the miscommunication; this is what "interferes" with Rose's communication. Bill and Rose both believe—falsely, as it turns out—that they share enough information to successfully communicate on this topic. Even though they are each acting in good faith, in reality they do not have sufficient common ground for successful communication here. Rose's intended meaning fails to be communicated to Bill.

In sum, insufficient common ground interferes with Bill's recognition of Rose's intended meaning and Rose's communication attempt fails. *Yard Sign* involves communicative failure and is thus a potential case of silencing.

§ 4.1.4 Why Should We Care?

OK so Rose is here silenced. Why should we care? After all, Rose herself doesn't seem to care too much about her ability to communicate with Bill. She realizes that he misunderstands her and she just walks away from him. For this reason, it might seem that this particular instance of silencing does not matter so much.

That might be right but let's not be too hasty. First, let's alter the case a bit. Suppose that Rose is a conservative student at a university where she is outnumbered by liberals. In a context like that, relevantly similar miscommunications would matter a lot more. Rose's professors and peers would routinely misunderstand her; she might also be vilified as a result of their errors. Rose's awareness of all of this would likely lead to anxiety, distraction, energy drain, underperformance, and ultimately undermine her educational experience. In a case like this, the miscommunications matter a lot more.[4]

Second, the kind of miscommunication involved in *Yard Sign* can go both ways. In *Yard Sign*, a liberal misinterprets a conservative, but these sorts of misunderstandings can certainly go the other way. I can tell you from personal experience interacting with my husband's family that conservatives misinterpret liberals, too.

Third, there is reason to believe that these sorts of miscommunications (between people with different political views) are really quite common. After all, it stands to reason that people with different political views will hold different background beliefs *and* be wrong about the background beliefs of those with different views. As a result, this sort of miscommunication happens a lot.

Fourth, these miscommunications often go undetected. This is because of what's called meta-ignorance. Ignorance is not knowing something. Meta-ignorance is ignorance about your own ignorance; in other words, to be meta-ignorant is to not know what you don't know. In *Yard Sign*, it is precisely because Bill is unaware of his being unaware (of criticisms of the BLM yard sign movement) that he misunderstands Rose *and* this is what causes Bill to be unaware of his misunderstanding. Remember that Bill left the conversation sincerely believing that he got it right.

Fifth, that this sort of thing happens so often should really trouble us. It's very bad for our democracy. How are we to collectively deliberate about issues of public concern if we are routinely misunderstanding one another? The situation is made even worse because these misunderstandings tend to lead to (unproductive) outrage and indignation.[5]

So, even if we think that the particular miscommunication between Rose and Bill in *Yard Sign* does not matter that much, the phenomenon of miscommunication across political difference does and should matter.

§ 4.1.5 Additional Lessons

There are several further points worth making explicit about this case. First, miscommunication—even really serious miscommunication like that between Rose and Bill—can happen even when the speaker and the hearer are acting in good faith. In *Yard Sign*, Bill tried to get it right and he honestly thought that he had. For her part, Rose expected Bill to understand her; she thought he knew stuff he didn't know but she thought she had a reasonable expectation that he did know. As you can see, hearers have a responsibility to interpret speakers charitably, and speakers have a responsibility to say what will enable the hearer to work out what is meant. In this case, Bill and Rose each did these things but an unrecognized lack of common ground nevertheless prevented successful communication.

Second, being aware of this possibility (namely, that common ground is lacking) brings with it an invitation, and even a responsibility. If we seek to avoid this kind of miscommunication, then we really ought to take special care to prevent it from happening. This means that when we are communicating with someone who is different from us (in some way that might lead to that person having different background beliefs) then we should take special care. We should be aware of the fact that there might be an absence of common ground and do what we can to facilitate mutual understanding.

Third, doing this will require staying open to the possibility that we might be missing something; it requires, that is, that we be aware of our own potential ignorance, and we are therefore just a bit humbler in our interactions with one another. If Bill had been more aware of the possibility that he was missing something important in his interactions with Rose, for example, things might have gone differently. Rather than experience full on horror by what he took her to mean, he might have asked for clarification instead. He might have said something like, "Hang on, Rose. What do you mean by that? Do you think that police brutality along racial lines isn't a thing?" and it could have gone from there. In suggesting this, I grant that we do not always have the energy or time to engage with one another in this way. And, political differences can also run a lot deeper. When they do, they are quite a bit more difficult to uncover.

In *Yard Sign*, Bill misunderstood Rose's speaker meaning but there are other kinds of interpretive mistakes regarding meaning that are also possible.[6] A hearer can misidentify the words actually uttered. A friend of mine—for most of his life actually—interpreted Mick Gilder's song "Hot Child in the City" as 'hot chocolate on the ceiling'. Another friend parsed 'Joycean stream' as 'joy-seeing stream'.[7]

We can also correctly identify the sound but misidentify the word or literal meaning of the word. For more years than I am willing to admit, I misidentified the meaning of one word in Elton John's "Goodbye Yellow Brick Road". The line is: 'I've finally decided my future lies beyond the yellow brick road'. I interpreted 'lies' as a noun, and wondered why the narrator planned to tell falsehoods once he got where he wanted to go. I found it perplexing (and even potentially deep) but my confusion wasn't enough to cause me to recognize my mistake! These sorts of mishaps are fairly common, and the science behind them is interesting.[8]

In this section, we have focused on ways in which the content or meaning of a speech act can be misidentified. When we speak, we do more than communicate content; we also perform actions. In the following section, we shall consider a different example; this one is less focused on content and more focused on the speech action being performed or attempted.

§ 4.2 Case 2: Messing Up the Speech Action

Remember that, in addition to communicating content, we also use speech to perform actions like apologizing, promising, threatening, refusing, consenting, proposing, and objecting. And, just as meaning can go unrecognized, so can these speech actions. When they do, it involves a different kind of recognition failure.[9] To illustrate, let's jump right into an example.

§ 4.2.1 The Case: *Graduate Seminar*

This case is called *Graduate Seminar*. The setting is a philosophy seminar in a top Ph.D. program in the United States. Margaret, John, Kevin, and Jim are students in the seminar. They are discussing a certain objection to Russell's theory of definite descriptions. Russell's theory specifies the conditions that must obtain in order for certain (kinds of) sentences to be true. According to Russell, the sentence 'the present king of France is bald' is true so long as 1. there is a present king of France, 2. there is only one king of France and 3. that king is bald. One (rather famous) objection to Russell's theory concerns the second condition, sometimes called the uniqueness condition. This requirement seems to get the wrong answer a lot of the time. Consider, for example, the sentence 'the desk is wooden.' In order for that sentence to be true, according to Russell's theory, it must be the case that 1. there is a desk, 2. there is only one desk, and 3. that desk is wooden. On Russell's analysis, the sentence 'the desk is wooden' will be false in any case where there is more than one desk. The students are discussing this problem (for Russell's theory) when the following exchange takes place:

KEVIN: Yeah, I get it; that's a problem.
JOHN: Uniqueness seems to work better for kings than for desks.
JIM: We could restrict the scope of the quantifier, but I don't know how Russell could do that without helping himself to indexicals.
MARGARET: Yes, but why focus just on truth? Why isn't it enough if both speaker and hearer have the same desk in mind?

KEVIN: Russell was very clearly concerned with the truth
              conditions. Look here [pointing to the text of "On
              Denoting".]
JIM: Yes, it's definitely about truth for Russell.
              Kevin, Jim, and John all nod in agreement.
              Margaret sighs.

§ 4.2.2 Analyzing the Case

In *Graduate Seminar*, Kevin, Jim, and John misunderstand Margaret. Let's focus on that misunderstanding. When
Margaret said, "Yes but why focus just on truth? Why isn't it
enough if both speaker and hearer have the same desk in mind?"
she intended to be objecting to Russell's enterprise. She knew
that Russell was concerned with truth and truth conditions,
but she was suggesting that an exclusive focus on truth might
be misguided. Without getting too bogged down in the philosophical details, Margaret was suggesting that communication
is what matters most when using language (and not the truth
or falsity of what is said), so when people actually use the sentence 'the desk is wooden' and both the speaker and the hearer
have the same desk in mind, they can successfully communicate
with one another about that desk exactly because they have that
same desk in mind. On Margaret's line of thinking, technical
details about reference and truth conditions are beside the point
for real-life practical purposes. For what it is worth, Margaret's
objection anticipates Donnellan's referential use of definite
descriptions, one of the most famous and influential responses
to Russell's theory.

Kevin, Jim, and John misinterpret Margaret's main point. They
take her to be confused about Russell's theory and why they are
talking about truth conditions while discussing it.[10] Her fellow
graduate students believe that Margaret is merely in need of

clarification about Russell's project. In this respect, they are mistaken; Margaret understands the truth-focused nature of Russell's project; what she says is an objection to that aspect of Russell's project. Kevin, Jim, and John misunderstand Margaret's objection by taking it as a request for an explanation.

Casey Johnson has argued that this sort of thing happens fairly often.[11] A woman says something involving expertise. That expertise goes unrecognized; she is interpreted as requesting information; then, the man "explains" things to her. And, when the woman has considerably more expertise on the topic than the man, it's ironic; it's also called 'mansplaining'. Rebecca Solnit is credited with first writing about this phenomenon.[12]

The primary interpretive mistake, in *Graduate Seminar*, concerns the speech action being performed. Margaret is here objecting as opposed to requesting clarification. Her fellow graduate students fail to recognize this. And, because they fail to recognize her speech action of objecting, they further misidentify her speaker meaning.[13] Kevin, Jim, and John fail to realize that Margaret is talking about the importance of communication as opposed to reference and truth.

§ 4.2.3 Is It Silencing?

Now, it is time to consider whether the interpretive mistake in *Graduate Seminar* counts as silencing. In particular, we need to decide whether it involves communicative failure, our one required condition of silencing.

In considering this question, we should mark a distinction. There are (at least) two mistakes here. First, Kevin, Jim, and John mistake an objection for a request for clarification. Then, as a result, they misidentify what Margaret is talking about; they misunderstand her speaker meaning. Now, we have already talked about (in the previous section) how the misidentification of speaker meaning can be silencing. For this reason, we will focus here on the misidentification of the speech action.

Is a speaker silenced when the addressees are mistaken about the speech action being performed? Yes, this is because, when this happens, communication fails. After all, exactly because Kevin, Jim, and John do not recognize that Margaret is objecting, her linguistic act of doing so is not successfully communicated to them. *Graduate Seminar* therefore involves communicative failure, our necessary condition for silencing.

§ 4.2.4 Why Should We Care?

OK but should we care about having our linguistic actions recognized? Does it matter all that much for Margaret that her objection goes unrecognized in *Graduate Seminar*? Arguably, it does and it does for several reasons. First, there is something that Margaret really ought to be able to do that she is prevented from doing (namely communicate her objection). Moreover, communicating objections is a crucially important part of philosophical discussions!

Second, Margaret is not being given credit for the philosophical insight that her remarks provide. As mentioned above, what she says anticipates an important move in the literature. That her fellow students fail to recognize the import of what she says does a disservice both to her and to their collective exploration and understanding of the issues. That they misunderstand her impoverishes their discussion and undermines everyone's educational experience.

Third, this mistake happens because Kevin, Jim, and John underestimate Margaret. If you are in any doubt about this, imagine that the professor had said what Margaret did. If the professor had said it, there is no way that the students would interpret the professor the way Kevin, Jim, and John interpreted Margaret (that is, as confused about why they were talking about truth conditions and as fundamentally confused about that nature of Russell's program). That they interpreted Margaret this way signals that they are disposed to think she is seriously confused and (probably also) not very good at philosophy. Thus, by understanding Margaret in the way that they did, her peers are also insulting her. And, having one's intellect insulted in an educational setting is not just non-ideal, it's potentially harmful.

Fourth, it's certainly possible that gender bias is playing a significant role in *Graduate Seminar*. It could well be, that is, that Margaret's male peers underestimate her precisely because she is a woman. If this is what is happening, then it is not an idiosyncratic mistake; it's part of a system of sexism, and it's likely to happen to Margaret at other times, to other women, and in plenty of other contexts. If this is what is happening, then the communicative failure is both systematic and group-based and these further features warrant additional concern.

§ 4.2.5 Additional Lessons

Before moving on, there are two features of this case worth highlighting at this point. The first concerns a reinforcement phenomenon. Notice that Kevin, Jim, and John underestimate Margaret. This causes them to misinterpret her in a way that prevents them from recognizing the import of what she says. Since what she says is an insightful objection, their mistake prevents them from recognizing evidence that they are wrong to operate with a low opinion of her. In short, their bias is reinforcing itself; it is causing mistakes that prevent them from detecting and correcting their errors. This kind of reinforcement mechanism is no doubt familiar to some of you. It is a very widespread phenomenon, and it masks and thus perpetuates many forms of bias.

Graduate Seminar concerns a failure to communicate an objection during a philosophical discussion but this kind of interpretive mistake can certainly undermine other kinds of linguistic actions. Speakers can also be silenced in this way when their apologies, promises, orders, or refusals go unrecognized. And, it does not take much to see that a failure to communicate these sorts of speech actions can have serious, lasting, and harmful consequences.

§ 4.3 Messing Up Sincerity

Thus far, we have considered examples that involve the hearer misunderstanding the speaker's intended meaning and the speech action being performed. We shall now consider a case that involves a different kind of recognition failure. It involves mistaking a sincere utterance for an insincere one.[14]

§ 4.3.1 The Case: *Fake Girl*

This case is called *Fake Girl*. Tom and Phil are both seniors at the local high school; they also live on the same street and ride the bus together. They have known each other their entire lives and their parents are close friends but Tom and Phil operate in different social circles at school. Tom is a football player and he hangs with the athletes; Phil works on the yearbook. Although they are not friends in school, they are friends outside of school.

Lately, Tom has been telling Phil a lot about a field hockey player named Sarah. Tom had a crush on Sarah but it did not work out. Tom now really regrets ever thinking well of Sarah; he now thinks that she is a total phony. With a clearer picture of her true character, Tom tells Phil that Sarah only really cares about being liked by the most popular kids and that she will say whatever she thinks will make them like her. He also says that she is really manipulative; he says that although she acts like she is really nice, she will go out of her way to raise a person's expectations just to dash them. He thinks she gets some sick pleasure out of hurting people.

Phil is disappointed to learn these things about Sarah because he had liked her; he had thought that she was one of the few decent "popular" girls; she'd always been nice to him and she was once really nice to his younger sister, Carla, when Sarah and Carla were in the Brownies together.

While waiting in the lunch line at school, Phil gets a text from Carla asking him to pick her up after school. Phil really can't go get her that day because he needs to take a make-up exam after school. Sarah is with him in the lunch line, and the following exchange takes place:

PHIL: Shit. [sigh]

SARAH: What is it?

PHIL: My sister needs a ride home but I can't go get her.

SARAH: [quizzical look]

PHIL: I have to take that f'in civics test today. It's today or no go. Billings is so unbelievably rigid.

SARAH: [smile in acknowledgement of his expressed frustration with Billings, the civics teacher] She goes to Memorial, right?

PHIL: Yeah.

SARAH: I could totally go get her. I'll be over that way anyway.
        [One of Sarah's friends walks up to her.]

PHIL: [gasp] Oh, wow. That's awesome. Really? You sure?

SARAH: Yeah. No worries. I promise. [Sarah starts to turn away from Phil and then says] And she'll remember me from Brownies.

After immediately feeling relieved at having his problem seemingly solved, Phil soon realizes that he cannot count on Sarah. In light of everything he learned about her from Tom, Phil quickly realizes that he needs to make other arrangements. So, Phil calls his mom at work. His mom agrees to pick Carla up; Phil then texts Carla back to tell her that their mom will come get her; he also tells his sister why he cannot.

Sarah arrives at the Memorial School just as Carla's mom is meeting her. Sarah is annoyed to discover that Carla already had a ride. Carla's mother, who left work early to go get her daughter, is annoyed to discover that doing so was completely unnecessary. Carla is miffed too. She has to deal with her mother venting during the entire ride home. Now, Sarah, Carla, and Phil's mom are each mad at Phil.

§ 4.3.2 Analyzing the Case

Let's focus on Sarah's promise to Phil. When Sarah said, "I promise," she was making a promise to Phil. In particular, Sarah was undertaking an obligation (to Phil) to give Carla a ride home from the Memorial School that day.

Phil realizes that Sarah is making a promise. He is in no doubt about the kind of speech action that her saying 'I promise' is. But, although Phil recognizes that she is promising (to give Carla a ride home that day), he nevertheless does not believe that Sarah has any intention of following through on that promise. In short, Phil takes Sarah to be insincere in her promise. He believes that she does not intend to keep the promise and that is why he thought he could not rely on her to do so.

§ 4.3.3 Is It Silencing?

Our job now is to decide whether this case involves silencing. In particular, we need to decide whether this kind of interpretive mistake involves communicative failure.

Recall from Chapter 3 that we had three conceptions of communicative failure; two of them are relevant here. The strict conception requires communication to fail because something the speaker intends to communicate—in the strict meta-intentional sense—is not recognized by the addressee. The impact conception, by contrast, requires only that the communication fails to have the impact in the world that it ought to have.

Focusing on the strict conception for a moment, we need to decide whether an addressee's failure to recognize a speaker's sincerity constitutes communicative failure in the strict sense. (Recall the discussion in § 3.4.) Remember that communicative intentions are complex ones that involve meta-intentions (that is, intentions about intentions). A speaker's sincerity is part of what is communicated only if the speaker has these sorts of complex communicative intentions about their own sincerity. Arguably, with some speech acts, and at least some of the time, speakers do have such intentions. When one promises, for example, it's plausible to suppose that sometimes a speaker actually intends to communicate (in this technical sense) both that one is promising and also that one really means it (that is, that one is sincere). For a case in point, recall *Reassuring Promise* from § 3.4.

Applying all of this to *Fake Girl*, if Sarah speaker means her sincerity, then this case involves *strict* communicative failure. This is because Tom does not recognize part of what Sarah intends to communicate in the strict sense, that is, her own sincerity.

Suppose, however, that, unaware of what Tom is saying about her, Sarah does not take her sincerity to be much of an issue and so she does not here speaker mean her sincerity; it is thus not within the scope of her communicative intentions.[15] In such a case, Phil's failure to recognize her sincerity would not be communicative failure in the strict sense.

So let's now consider the impact conception of communicative failure. Might Phil's failure to recognize Sarah's sincerity prevent her promise from having the worldly impact that it ought to have? Yes, it seems it certainly can. In fact, it might even prevent the very effect, the production of which, is Sarah's main reason for performing the promise in the first place. Arguably, Sarah's main purpose in making this promise to Phil was to reassure and help him. Phil was in a bind and Sarah's promise offered a way out of that bind. But, Phil's failure to recognize Sarah's sincerity prevented her promise from doing either of these things. Since Phil did not believe that she meant it, her promise did not de-stress him. Exactly because Phil thought he could not rely on her promise, he did not rely on it and he frantically went ahead and made other arrangements. And, because Phil's mom picked Carla up from school, Sarah did not get a chance to help Phil out by driving Carla home that day. In this way, we see that Phil's mistake about Sarah's sincerity prevents Sarah's promise from doing the two things she aimed to do with it (that is, de-stress Phil and help him out). Phil's sincerity mistake thus prevents Sarah's promise from having the impact that it aims to have and that it ought to have. Interpreted this way, *Fake Girl* thus constitutes impact communicative failure. As a result, it's a potential instance of silencing.

§ 4.3.4 Why Should We Care?

Phil's interpretive mistake in *Fake Girl* certainly leads to regrettable outcomes. Sarah is insulted and her time is wasted. Phil's mom misses work when that sacrifice could have easily been avoided. Carla is annoyed because she has to listen to her mom complain during the drive home and she also has to deal with the tension in the household that evening. Phil, who is arguably just trying to be a responsible son and brother, ends up with everybody mad at him. Everyone seems to lose in *Fake Girl*.

It is worth pointing out that Phil's interpretive mistake here could lead to harm, in addition to annoyance and frustration. Phil's mom might lose pay or get a bad evaluation at work (leading to reduced professional stature and ultimately reduced compensation). Sarah might develop anxiety upon discovering the sorts of things that are being said about her (and the seeming impossibility of setting the record straight). Phil's relationships (with Tom and Sarah) might also be harmed.

Another reason to care about *Fake Girl* concerns the possibility that gender is playing a significant role here. It could be that Tom expected Sarah to be romantically available to him and when she was not he felt injured because he felt entitled.[16] It could also be that Phil was inclined to believe these things about Sarah because they square with negative stereotypes about girls and women being insincere and manipulative by nature. If either of these things is true, then the interpretive mistake in *Fake Girl* is no accident; it's group-based and systematic. As such, it's part of a broader social pattern and that pattern disadvantages women and girls. Seen in this light, the seemingly ordinary interpretive mistake that (potentially) silences Sarah in *Fake Girl* could also be part of a sinister system of sexism.

Making matters even worse, such sincerity silencing, as some call it, can affect speech acts other than promises.[17] If sincere assertions are not recognized as such, then they are taken to be lies, and when this happens, the assertion is not believed and (arguably) the speaker is maligned as a liar. Also extremely troubling is the potential sincerity silencing of refusals. If a refusal is taken as insincere, that refusal is highly unlikely to be respected. Since the main purpose of refusing is to have one's refusal respected, a failure to recognize the speaker's sincerity interferes with the main purpose and function of a refusal. This possibility is especially worrying in the case of sexual refusals.[18]

§ 4.3.5 Additional Lessons

Another feature of the silencing phenomenon in *Fake Girl* is worthy of additional reflection: third-party interference. In *Fake*

Girl, there is miscommunication between Sarah and Phil but someone else caused it. It's what Tom said about Sarah that causes the problem; Tom's claims about Sarah's character and motivations (coupled with Phil believing him) interfered with Phil's recognition of Sarah's sincerity. Tom, who is a third party to the communication in question (between Phil and Sarah), causes the communicative failure.

Such third-party interference played a crucial role in a famous legal case in England: *DPP v. Morgan*.[19] Sparing the reader all the upsetting details, here is the gist of that case. Morgan invited three men to his home to have sex with his wife. According to those three men (but not according to Morgan), Morgan had told them that his wife would pretend to refuse and that any signs of a struggle were really just part of the role-play in a consensual and kinky plan. Morgan allegedly also told the men that his wife would enjoy it and that she wanted him to bring some men home to have sex with her.[20] If the defense is to be believed here, Morgan's lies about his wife interfered with those men recognizing the sincerity of her refusals.[21]

It is well worth mentioning at this point that there has been a lot of discussion in feminist writings about the possibility that some pornography might constitute this kind of third-party communicative interference. According to some theorists, (some) pornography portrays women in ways that interfere with women's ability to communicate; the idea is that consuming these kinds of pornography alters consumers' beliefs in ways that lead to the very sorts of interpretive mistakes that silence. Exploring this is now a huge literature.[22] And, it's one influential way of understanding what Catharine MacKinnon meant when she (famously) claimed that pornography silences women and violates women's right to free speech.[23]

On a (potentially) lighter note, Alan Funt, who was the host of a popular television program in the 1970s that featured playing practical jokes on unsuspecting members of the public, was on an airplane that had been hijacked. Because Funt was on board, the passengers on the plane thought it was a practical joke and did not believe that the hijackers were sincere. This actually happened.[24] Thankfully, the plane landed safely, and no one on board was physically hurt.

§ 4.4 Additional Recognition Failures

Thus far, we have considered three ways that a communication attempt can go wrong. Each of these ways involves the addressee failing to recognize some aspect of the attempted communication. In this section, I will identify three additional recognition failures. But, in the interest of space, that is all that I will do.

§ 4.4.1 Speaker Authority

Some additional recognition failures concern speaker authority. After all, some speech actions require that the speaker have authority. When a person orders someone to do something, when a parent enacts a new bedtime, when a teacher offers an extension, and when a jury renders a verdict, the speakers in these cases have, and are exercising, the authority to do these things. It's possible for an addressee to fail to recognize that the speaker has the requisite authority and it is also possible for an addressee, who recognizes that the speaker has the requisite authority, to fail to recognize that the speaker is exercising that authority on the occasion in question. Let's look at some cases.

Sexual Refusal: Authority Version: Meg is a sex worker. During her encounter with a client, Chuck, Meg says no intending to refuse and thus put an authoritative end to their encounter. Although Chuck recognizes Meg's intention to refuse, he nevertheless believes that she is unable to do so because he has already paid her.

Adjourning Department Meeting: Alison is the department chair. After three hours discussing whether or not an Oxford comma belongs in a particular sentence in an inconsequential memo to the dean, Alison throws up her hands in exasperation and says, "I just can't take this anymore. Meeting Adjourned!" Her colleagues know that, as chair, she has the power to end the meeting but they take her to be cracking a joke instead.[25]

These cases illustrate two ways that a speaker's authority can go unrecognized. In *Sexual Refusal: Authority Version*, the addressee, Chuck, falsely believes that Meg does not have the authority to refuse, so although he recognizes her intention to do so, he nevertheless believes that she cannot refuse him. The recognition failure is a bit different in *Adjourning Department Meeting*. There, the colleagues know that Alison has the power to end the meeting, it's just that, on this occasion, they think that she is cracking a joke so they fail to realize that she is, in fact, exercising her authority in order to terminate the meeting.

Again, I won't take the space to explore these sorts of interpretive mistakes in further detail here but these issues are gaining attention in the philosophical literature.[26]

§ 4.4.2   Reason for Speech Act

Another way for a speech act to go awry concerns the addressee's beliefs about what is motivating the speaker. Once again, examples will help.

Paul's Promise: Paul publicly promises Tim that he will donate money to the school fund drive. Tim mistakenly believes that

Paul's primary reason for doing so is to impress a woman Paul hopes to date.

Sexual Refusal: Propriety Version: Meg says no to Chuck and, in so doing, Meg sincerely intends to be refusing Chuck's sexual advances. Although Chuck recognizes Meg's sincere intention to refuse him, he nevertheless incorrectly believes that she is only doing so because she wants to be regarded as a morally good woman.

In each of these cases, the addressee appears to recognize the intended meaning, the speech action performed, and the speaker's sincerity but the addressee nevertheless holds a false belief about what is motivating the speaker to perform the speech act in question.

§ 4.4.3 True Self

We shall consider just one more way that an attempted communication can go awry; it involves the addressee falsely believing that the speaker is self-deceived or not in full control of their speech actions. Examples will help to make this type of mistake easier to grasp.

PMS: Harriet is furious with her husband Peter, who seems constitutionally incapable of wiping a kitchen counter. As she patiently explains to him yet again how frustrating it is for her to have to clean up after him (and to have to do so in order to cook dinner for everyone after a long work day), he dismisses her concerns. He figures she's on her period and this is just the PMS (premenstrual syndrome) talking.[27]

Sexual Refusal: True Self Version: Laurel says no to Hudson and, in so doing, she sincerely intends to be refusing Hudson's sexual advances. Although Hudson recognizes Laurel's sincere intention to refuse him, he nevertheless incorrectly believes that she is sexually repressed and that her true self wants their encounter. He also mistakenly believes that she will shortly come to realize this herself.

In each of these cases, the addressee falsely believes that the speech action performed is not in keeping with what the speaker truly wants. Sometimes, this leads an addressee to view the speech action as entirely outside of the speaker's will, and thus as something that the speaker—in some important sense—isn't really doing. Mark Schroeder calls this 'attributive silencing'.[28]

§ 4.5 On Social Scripts and Seriousness

This section offers a bit of a deeper dive. Readers who just want an overview of silencing options might elect to skip straight to Chapter 5.

Laura Caponetto has drawn attention to something that she calls 'seriousness silencing'.[29] It's really interesting and worth a closer look. But, while I agree with Caponetto's insight that seriousness silencing is a distinct phenomenon, I disagree with some of her claims about it.

Let's get started. Most speaking contexts are serious ones.[30] This means that the presumption is that speakers are committing to what they are saying and they are performing the speech acts that they appear to be performing. But, not all contexts are like this. Sometimes, the presumption of seriousness is lifted. To see this, consider the following:

Joking: Terry and Jack are brothers who enjoy a somewhat competitive tradition of joke-telling. They aim to master this craft and outdo each other with respect to timing, tone, and originality. One day, Terry starts a narrative joke, "a turtle, a horse, and a dirty pigeon walk into the clubhouse at Gooseberry Beach and ... "

Actor: Latisha is an actor in a play. In a particularly poignant conversation with her character's best friend, Molly, Latisha describes childhood trauma and how it has led to so much of her adult pain and dysfunction.

In each of these cases, the presumption of seriousness is suspended.[31] In *Joking*, Terry is not actually asserting that a turtle, a horse, and a dirty pigeon walked into the clubhouse. What Terry says is part of the joke-narrative; it's a kind of fiction. Whatever else is going on here, Terry is not committing to the truth of what he is here saying. So, too in *Actor*. Latisha is acting out her lines, but she is not really sharing about her actual life. She is in character. And, while her character might be making these claims, Latisha, the actor, is not.

Consider now an example made famous by Donald Davidson and discussed by several in the silencing literature.[32]

Fire Warning: While on stage performing in a play, an actor notices that a fire has broken out in the rear of the theater. When the actor tries to warn the audience about the fire, they interpret his warning as part of the play.

In her classic work on silencing, Rae Langton discusses this example and treats it as an instance of illocutionary uptake failure (which it is).[33] The actor's illocutionary intention to warn (about the fire) is not recognized by the audience members. They take him to be acting and not to be warning at all.

Caponetto argues that this case is importantly different from other cases of illocutionary uptake failure.[34] To draw out the difference, consider the following.

Speed Trap: Greg routinely drives on North Street to get to work. John tries to warn him when he says to Greg, "There have been a lot of police with radar guns in the park n' ride lot lately." Greg appreciates the information because, as a town selectman, he has an interest in town activities and thus in the public's awareness of town police presence. Greg takes John to be sharing information about this but not as warning him.

In *Speed Trap*, John is intending to warn Greg but Greg fails to recognize that illocutionary intention. This is a case of illocutionary uptake recognition failure but it is different from what is happening in *Fire Warning*. In *Fire Warning*, the actor is attempting to warn but is misinterpreted as still merely acting in the play, that is, as being in a non-serious context. This is not the situation in *Speed Trap*. There, Greg takes John to be in a serious speech context; it's just that he fails to correctly identify John's illocutionary intention. Caponetto is thus correct in pointing out that there is this important difference.[35]

In analyzing this difference, however, Caponetto claims that when a speaker in a serious context is misinterpreted as being in a non-serious context, that speaker is taken as not illocuting at all.[36] I disagree; non-serious speech acts are speech acts; it's just that they are considerably more complex speech acts.[37] As I will now show, speakers in such contexts are, contra Caponetto, illocuting and, moreover, they are interpreted as illocuting.

Before arguing for this, though, it makes sense to first explore a clear and uncontroversial case of a "speaker" who is not illocuting at all. To that end, consider the following example.

AI: An AI machine produces computer-generated verbalization in response to textual inputs that are randomly generated.

In *AI*, the sounds produced by the AI machine are not illocutions at all; this is because there are no communicative intentions whatsoever involved in the case. So, even if the machine says, "Really, there's a fire in the back of the theater", we will not take it as a warning; we will not take it as any sort of speech act at all and we would be right to do so. Contrast this with what is happening in either *Fire Warning* or in *Actor*. These cases are different; unlike the AI machine, actors do have communicative intentions. Moreover, audiences know this and interpret actors' speech actions accordingly. It's just that these speech actions are not straightforward ones; as we shall now see, they are quite complex.

Consider *Actor* again. While it is true that Latisha is not actually performing the assertions that she purports to be performing in the fiction of the play,[38] she is nevertheless—and quite obviously—performing communicative acts; this means that Latisha is illocuting. Moreover, audience members interpret Latisha as illocuting. We learn from Latisha's performance. This much is clear.

What is less clear, however, is precisely how to understand Latisha's speech actions. Regrettably, I will not be offering anything like a full analysis. Instead, I offer some general observations.

First, Latisha's speech action involves multiple audiences and different forms of indirection. The other actors on the stage are one audience and the people watching the play are another. This multiplicity of audience involves indirection. Although Latisha addresses the actor playing Molly, her primary audience is really the set of theater-goers.[39] As Stephen Levinson stresses, when a lawyer questions a witness, the primarily intended audience is really the jury, and not the addressee, who is the witness on the stand.[40] Although court proceedings are a kind of performance, it would be a mistake to think that lawyers are not—and are not taken as—illocuting at all.

Second, non-serious utterances seem to involve what Herbert Clark and Thomas Carlson call 'informatives'; these are speech actions that inform participants about the speech actions being performed.[41] Informatives are subtle so an example will help.

> *Triad*: Katie, Maeve, and Nora are having a conversation. At a
> certain point in that conversation, Maeve turns to Katie and
> Maeve promises Katie to pick her up in New York on her way
> back to Maryland.

In *Triad*, Nora recognizes Maeve's promise to Katie and—
importantly—Maeve intends for Nora to recognize that promise
to Katie. This is so even though Nora is not the addressee; Katie
is. Despite this, Maeve fully intends for Nora to hear and to recognize her promise to Katie; in other words, as a participant in this
conversation, Nora is an intended overhearer of Maeve's promise.
According to Clark and Carlson, Maeve has a communicative intention *towards Nora* that informs Nora of Maeve's promise to
Katie. This is the informative speech act.[42]

If Clark and Carlson are correct, then informative speech acts
are ubiquitous. They are also present in non-serious contexts
and this is plain to see. When Latisha's character spills her guts
to Molly on stage, Latisha, the actor, intends to inform the audience about the speech actions her character is performing in the
play. By performing these informatives, Latisha, the actor, is
illocuting. Similarly, when reading a book aloud, the speaker might
not be asserting the book's content, but that speaker is nevertheless illocuting; that speaker is informing their audience about that
content.[43]

Second, a compelling case can be made that, in addition to
these informatives, at least some of the background assumptions
of fictional content are in fact asserted in fictional (non-serious)
contexts.[44] David Lewis, for example, famously claims that there
is "truth in fiction". According to Lewis, in any fiction, there is a
purportedly factual background to the fictional foreground and
these background facts are sometimes asserted.[45] Applying this
to *Actor*, while the specifics of Latisha's character's experience are
not asserted, some presuppositions nevertheless seem to be. In
particular, Latisha's monologue seems to assert that some children

experience trauma and that such trauma has lasting effects well into adulthood.[46]

Third, and despite the informative and assertoric illocutionary aspects of Latisha's monologue, we might nevertheless regard its primary purpose as perlocutionary. On this line of thinking, the primary purpose of Latisha's speech action is to elicit an emotional-aesthetic response in the audience.

With all this in hand, let's now get back to Caponetto's serious-ness silencing and the kind of case that concerns her.

Social Script: After a lovely evening out and as things start to get physical, Tina says "not yet, Lou; I'm not ready" intending to put an end to their sexual encounter. Lou interprets Tina as merely following a social script, according to which women make as if to refuse and they do so several times before it is socially acceptable to consent.

In *Social Script*, Lou does not interpret Tina as refusing; instead, he interprets her as giving voice to her lines in a social ritual of a certain kind. These social rituals are common. When greeting strangers on a footpath, for example, it is not unusual to say, "Hi, how are you?" as you pass one another. When doing so, though, one is not actually posing a question; one is not, that is, asking for information regarding that stranger's wellbeing. Rather, one is per-forming a social ritual of greeting. One makes as if to inquire after their wellbeing in order to acknowledge their presence and greet them. These social rituals involve speech acts. In some cultures, there are similar scripts regarding offers of food. One must purport to decline a second helping several times before it would be appro-priate to accept. Clearly, social scripts of this kind are sometimes operative; we know how to participate in and interpret them, and they involve speech actions.

In *Social Script*, however, Lou makes a mistake; he gets it wrong; he thinks that Tina is simply following a social script when she is not just doing that.[47] Lou misinterprets Tina as merely going through the ritual motions, when, in actuality, she is sincerely refusing. This is a paradigmatic instance of Caponetto's seriousness silencing.[48]

So what should we make of seriousness silencing? No doubt it's an important phenomenon and it happens in real life. But is it silencing?

First, it's unlikely to be—all by itself—communicative failure in the strict sense. This is because speakers typically do *not* speaker-mean the seriousness of their speaking context. So unless a speaker is intending to communicate that the speaking context is a serious one, an addressee's failure to recognize the seriousness of a context does not constitute strict communicative failure.

That said, interpretive mistakes about seriousness will—in all likelihood—lead to *other* recognition failures that *do* constitute communicative failure, in the strict sense. To see this, let's consider *Social Script* again. Exactly because Lou falsely believes that Tina is merely following a social script when she purports to refuse him, Lou fails to recognize Tina's intention to sincerely refuse. Lou's mistake about the seriousness of Tina's speech action leads him to misinterpret her illocution in other ways. Moreover, these other ways do constitute communicative failure in the strict sense

Second, although speakers typically do not speaker intend the seriousness of their speaking context, it's certainly possible for seriousness silencing to be strict communicative failure. To see this, consider an altered version of *Social Script*.

> *Social Script Seriousness*: After a lovely evening out and as things start to get physical, Tina says "not yet, Lou; I'm not ready. This is no pretense; for now it's a no" intending to put an end to their sexual encounter. Tina is aware that some men think that women play act during sexual encounters so she says what she says in order to communicate to him that that is *not* what she is doing. Despite this, Lou still interprets Tina as merely following a social

script, according to which women are coy and make as if to refuse in order to heighten excitement and anticipation.

In *Social Script Seriousness*, Tina does speaker-mean the seriousness of her speaking context; part of what she wants to tell him is that she is not play acting and just following a social script. So, Lou's failure to recognize the seriousness of her speech action *does*, in this case, constitute communicative failure in the strict sense.

Third, a failure to recognize the seriousness of a speech action will typically prevent that speech action from having the effect in the world that it ought to have. Exactly because Lou fails to recognize the seriousness of Tina's utterance, he doesn't recognize that she is refusing, and this leads to his failure to respect that refusal. Tina's sincere refusals fail to do what refusals aim to do and ought to be able to do, that is, put an authoritative stop to their encounter.[49] This suggests that seriousness silencing will also lead to the impact version of communicative failure.

§ 4.6 Conclusion

Recognition failure silencing occurs when something interferes with either the communication of an attempted speech act (this involves strict communicative failure) or with the appropriate impact of an attempted speech act (this is impact prevention failure). I have here considered six different ways that an attempted speech act can go awry; each such way involves the addressee making a mistake and getting something important wrong.

In the next chapter, I explore another broad type of silencing. With this type of silencing, something prevents a communicative act from having the effect in the world that it ought to have.

5

Ineffectual Words

On Impact Prevention

In the previous chapter, I considered a variety of ways that a communication attempt can go awry because the intended recipient fails to recognize some important aspect of that communication. In this chapter, I look at something else. I look at ways that speech can be prevented from impacting the world the way that it should. So, even if a certain utterance is successful in a narrow technical sense of being successfully communicated, that utterance might nevertheless not bring about its warranted worldly effect. In thinking about this, it is important to keep in mind that there are lots of ways that language can and should affect the world. But, before we explore some of these other impacts, I first focus on one of the main things we do with language, namely share information.

When we share information with people—when we tell people things—we aim to change their beliefs. If for some reason, we are not believed, then our utterance is prevented from having its intended effect. This result might be as it should be. Not everyone is credible and we all make mistakes. That said, however, sometimes when a speaker is not believed, something has gone wrong. As we shall soon see, though, there are different sorts of cases involving a speaker not being believed; some involve recognition failures and some do not. In the next two sections, I spell out this difference.

On Silencing. Mary Kate McGowan, Oxford University Press. © Mary Kate McGowan 2026.
DOI: 10.1093/9780197837320.003.0005

§ 5.1 Case One of Not Being Believed

Consider the following case, based (loosely) on a real one.

Ed's Ribs: Ed is a middle-aged African American man who fell off a ladder, landed on his side, and sought medical attention. Describing the accident and his pain, the attendant does an X-ray, but sees nothing amiss. Ed is sent home and told to take Tylenol for any discomfort. The pain increases, so Ed goes to another facility, but receives the same result. When the pain continues to increase and Ed begins to have difficulty breathing, he goes to an Emergency Room. The staff there do an initial assessment and determine that Ed's case is low priority, so he is instructed to wait while more serious conditions are treated. After five hours at the Emergency Room, Ed is seen and it is discovered that he has three broken ribs and a collapsed lung.[1]

In this case, it is clear that Ed's injuries are not treated as seriously as they should be. His description of his accident, his pain reports, and his requests for medical attention go unheeded for quite some time. Why is this happening? What might be going on here? Here's what we know. The clinicians at the first two facilities looked at x-rays on film, inspected the film while it was still wet from the developing chemicals, and did not see any breaks or fractures; they then concluded that Ed did not have any broken ribs. The problem with treating the x-ray evidence this way is that it is a well-known medical fact that fractures often do not show up on an initial (wet) read of x-ray film and some fractures do not show up even when the film has dried. So, although the x-ray did not show that Ed *did* have a fracture, it should certainly *not* have been treated as evidence that he *did not* have a fracture. And, given what Ed told them about his accident and his pain, it seems that the clinicians should have taken Ed's condition more seriously.

OK so why didn't they? It's impossible to know for certain (because we cannot get inside the heads of those clinicians to directly see) what they were thinking. But here is a possibility that we have good reason to believe happens quite a bit: the clinicians might well have suspected that Ed was lying in order to get narcotics. Addicts are known to do this; they lie about being in pain in order to get a prescription for a pain killer. Clinicians are well aware of the phenomenon and try to avoid giving drugs when doing so is not medically warranted. Given how complex judgments about other people's pain reports are, clinicians are bound to sometimes get it wrong. And getting it wrong involves either denying medication to a person who is medically in need of it or giving drugs to an addict who is fraudulently acquiring them. Mistakes are inevitable and "honest" mistakes are understandable.

A worrying possibility—really a probability—is that some of these mistakes are driven by bias, whether conscious or not. There is good empirical evidence suggesting that social bias plays an important but illegitimate role in these judgments about whom to believe. Such studies show that people of color, for example, are significantly more likely to be suspected of this opioid-seeking behavior and, as a result, they are also more likely to be denied medically necessary pain medication.[2]

Bringing this back to issues of communication, Ed's claims (about being in an accident, hurting his chest, and being in significant pain) are not believed, and this is because the clinicians think that Ed is lying to them. In short, Ed's sincere claims are mistaken for insincere ones; this involves one of the kinds of recognition failure that we discussed in the previous chapter. We called it sincerity silencing.

Arguably, *Ed's Ribs* is an especially troubling case of sincerity silencing and there are several reasons for this. First, Ed's race contributes (even if only unconsciously) to the clinicians' suspicions and thus to Ed's being sincerity silenced. Ed is treated in this way because of his race, his group membership. Second and relatedly, Ed's being sincerity silenced is caused by racism; it also perpetuates racism. Third, this instance of sincerity silencing is especially harmful in the short run; after all, it prevents Ed from receiving adequate medical care and it prolongs his pain. Fourth and finally, it's likely to be "unshakable". This means that it is particularly difficult for Ed to overcome the sincerity silencing and have his sincere claims recognized as such. To see this, suppose that Ed realizes that the clinicians suspect that he is an addict. In that case, it's going to be really difficult for Ed to convince them otherwise. After all, whatever Ed does or says in an attempt to convince them is also something that a determined addict could do or say. In this way, the sincerity silencing in *Ed's Ribs* is especially pernicious.

This case also illustrates one way that different kinds of silencing can interact. In Ed's case, the recognition failure (of Ed's sincerity) leads to Ed's utterances not being believed so the sincerity silencing prevents his claims from effecting the world (that is, updating the clinicians' beliefs) as they should. Exactly because the health care workers think that Ed is lying to them, they do not believe what he says to them.

Going forward in this chapter, though, I will focus on cases of impact prevention that do *not* also involve recognition failure. That is, I will look at examples where the utterance is fully recognized— and so it succeeds communicatively—but it nevertheless fails to have the impact that it ought to have. It makes sense to focus on these sorts of cases too so that I can isolate distinct phenomena.

As we shall soon see, not all cases of a speaker not being believed are cases where the speaker is thought to be lying. The impact prevention here is not caused by a recognition failure; it's caused by something else. And, in my quest to understand the various ways that language use can be undermined, I should identify this other way too. To this end, I consider another case of not being believed, but this time, the speaker is not mistakenly thought to be insincere.

§ 5.2 Case Two of Not Being Believed

Here is the case. It too is based (loosely) on a real one.

> *Small Pox*: During a small pox epidemic in early eighteenth cen-
> tury Boston, an African enslaved person, called Onesimus, tells
> his owner, Cotton Mather, about a practice of inoculation that
> was widely and successfully used in West Africa to protect against
> small pox. Mather believes him, manages to convince a Boston
> doctor to try it but the general population at the time was highly
> skeptical, unwilling—it seems—to rely on the "superstitious"
> practices of such "primitive" cultures.[3]

In *Small Pox*, Onesimus isn't believed but it's not because skeptical Bostonians think that he is lying. No, this case is different from
what is happening in *Ed's Ribs*. The skeptical Bostonians believe
that Onesimus believes what Onesimus is saying. Instead, these
skeptics think Onesimus is mistaken. They trust Onesimus's sincerity, just not his judgment.

When people tell us things, we make judgments about the credibility of what we have been told. Plenty of considerations affect
these judgments. The content of what is said, the way it is said, and
who says it being chief among them. In *Small Pox*, Onesimus's assertion, as a piece of evidence, is given less weight than it should
be.[4] The Bostonians' prejudice against African cultures causes them
to illegitimately lower the credibility attributed to what Onesimus
reports.

In *Small Pox*, we don't have any of the kinds of recognition failures
that we explored in the last chapter. The skeptical Bostonians recognize what sort of speech act Onesimus is performing (that is, an
assertion); they recognize what Onesimus is telling him (that is,
that inoculation works against small pox), and they recognize that
Onesimus believes what he is saying. So, Onesimus's speech action
succeeds fully as a communicative act. The problem here is that

Onesimus's say so fails to have the evidential impact that it ought to have. Onesimus tried to share his knowledge with the community but was prevented from doing that because Onesimus's say so was not regarded as decent enough evidence.

§ 5.3 On Credibility and Knowledge Transmission

When you stop to think about it, the vast majority of what we believe is based on what other people tell us. Most of our knowledge is indirect in this way. We know that kangaroos live in Australia, for example, but most of us have never actually seen one there. In fact, most of us have never even been to Australia. We also know that George Washington was the first president of the United States but we do not know this directly; none of us even existed when he lived. The lion's share of what we know, we know indirectly, and thus by relying on others. When we learn from books, news stations, teachers, parents, friends, and so on, we are relying on what we have been told.

There is a sizable philosophical literature concerned with the transmission of knowledge through speech acts of telling, but for my purposes, three things matter most.[5] First, most of what we know, we know from being told in one way or another. So, the communicative act of telling people things is a—perhaps the—major distributor of knowledge. Second, when we tell people things, our act of telling them is offered as evidence of the truth of what we tell them.[6] When Nikki tells her colleague Jim about the meeting that was just scheduled, what she says functions as evidence for Jim. Nikki knows things; she tells those things to Jim, so that he can know them too. Jim now knows those things because he relies on Nikki's say so. Third and finally, when we are told things, we make complicated and very quick judgments about what we are being told; we quickly assess that speech act of telling as a piece of evidence; we make a very fast and complex judgment about the credibility of the speaker's claim.

When we judge the credibility of what we are being told, we consider several things simultaneously. We consider the content of what we are being told. If an elderly woman in the supermarket tells Charlotte that she just got back from an expedition to the moon, Charlotte is unlikely to believe this woman because what this elderly woman says is so implausible. Charlotte knows that elderly women are exceedingly unlikely to be astronauts. Charlotte's background beliefs ground her plausibility judgment of the content of what she is told and thus the credibility Charlotte gives to the elderly woman's statement. We also consider how we are being told. If someone seems nervous or uncertain, their demeanor might undermine the evidential weight of what that person is saying. Another thing we consider is the source, that is, we judge the credibility of the speaker. This judgment might be based on what we know about an individual person but it might also be based on assumptions about the speaker's social identity. A woman making expert claims about car repair, for example, might well be deemed less credible than a man making the same claims would be.

When making these judgments, we are bound to make mistakes. There are several reasons for this. As we just saw, these credibility judgments are especially complex; we have to make them really often, and we also have to do so virtually instantaneously. In light of these considerations, we are bound to sometimes get them wrong. Furthermore, when faced with complex decisions that need to be made often and quickly, we look for shortcuts, allowing ourselves to be guided by gut feelings and snap judgments. As a result, these credibility judgments are especially susceptible to various kinds of bias, including social bias. Given that these judgments are particularly likely to be influenced by prejudice, we should slow down and be on guard, if we want to increase the chances of getting them right.

We say that there is a 'credibility deficit' when a credibility judgment is lower than it should be and we say that there is a 'credibility excess' when a credibility judgment is higher than it should be. Both of these mistakes are problematic—and even potentially harmful—but, going forward, I will focus on credibility deficits.[7]

Perhaps unsurprisingly, this phenomenon (of speaker's not being given the credibility they deserve) has long drawn the attention of theorists, and it has done so in a variety of fields. Black Feminists, for example, have long discussed how the experiences of Black women are socially devalued.[8] Kristie Dotson has recently given the phenomenon a name; she calls it 'testimonial quieting'.[9] Feminist epistemologists and philosophers of science have long explored injustices in the social dimensions of knowledge production.[10] And, more recently, analytic feminists and epistemologists have also attended to the phenomenon. Miranda Fricker, for example, calls it 'testimonial injustice'.[11] These theorists tend to be concerned with credibility deficits that are group-based. This means that a speaker's testimony is devalued because that speaker is a member of a certain (typically marginalized) social group.

Credibility deficits can be harmful in a whole host of ways. First, any deflation of credibility undermines the flow of knowledge, and this, in turn, hampers the sharing of what we know. If knowledge is prevented from spreading as it should, then we collectively know less. In this way, credibility deficits impair the social accumulation of knowledge.

Second, the damage to shared knowledge is considerably worsened when credibility deficits are patterned in certain ways. We have already seen that there is good reason to believe that group-based prejudice plays a crucial role in devaluing the credibility of some social groups. And, when credibility deficits are group-based in this way, there is systematic devaluing of knowledge coming from whole groups of people. And, when legitimate sources of knowledge are curtailed in such a patterned way, our collective knowledge is further undermined. *Small Pox* is a case in point, where knowledge from Africans is systematically devalued and even dismissed.

Third, whenever there is a credibility deficit, the speaker is devalued as a knower.[12] So, there is an epistemic (that is, knowledge-based) harm to the speaker. To see this, consider again what happened in *Small Pox*. There, the Bostonians understand perfectly well what Onesimus is claiming, and they also recognize that Onesimus is sincere; in short, the skeptical Bostonians know that Onesimus believes what he is saying. But, although these Bostonians believe that Onesimus believes what he is saying, they nevertheless do not take the fact that Onesimus believes these things to be a good reason for them to believe them too or even to take the claims seriously; these Bostonians therefore devalue Onesimus as a source of knowledge; they devalue Onesimus as a testifier, as a knower, and as an epistemic agent.

Fourth, such group-based credibility deficits further undermine speakers who are already disadvantaged in terms of their social group membership. This is effectively a feedback loop that has compounding negative effects on some members of society more than others. (And this negativity is further—even exponentially—compounded for people occupying more than one socially disadvantaged group.)[13]

Fifth and finally, it's not just knowledge that is undermined. So is democracy. When entire groups of people have their claims devalued, those groups are less effective participants in political deliberation; they are less credible discussants of issues of public concern. These devalued groups are also less efficacious in their criticisms of government and in communicating their views to elected officials. All of these communicative capacities are crucial for a well-functioning democracy. So, to the extent that certain social groups are systemically inhibited in their political participation, a democracy is undermined. Arguably, so too is the very legitimacy of that democracy, which after all relies on the equal representation and participation of its populace.

That's a lot to absorb. And, for some readers, all of this is new. For others, it is an everyday lived experience. Thus far, I have focused on credibility deficits; I have focused on how acts of telling can be prevented from affecting the world as they should. Although telling is a very important kind of speech act, it is certainly not the only kind of utterance that can be undermined in this way. In the next section, I consider other sorts of impact, and I also clarify this notion of impact.

§ 5.4 More On Impact

In general, when we say things, we do so for a reason. We aim to achieve something. As we just saw, when we tell people things, we typically aim to share our knowledge with them. But there are other objectives involved with language use. When we apologize to someone, for example, it's usually because we seek to repair our relationship with that person. And, when we order, we do so in order to get others to do things. These other sorts of impacts can be undermined too.

Recall from Chapter 2 that Austin distinguished between three different forces of an utterance: the locutionary force, the illocutionary force, and the perlocutionary force. Pretty much every time we say something, our utterance has each of these three forces.[14] Let's make this concrete with an example.

> *Kitchen Fire*: Sam and Gavin are watching a Netflix show together in their living room when Sam notices the reflection of flames in their living room window. Quickly realizing what is happening, Sam jumps off the couch and yells "There is a fire in the kitchen!"

Sam's utterance ("There is a fire in the kitchen!") has all three of these forces. The locutionary force of what Sam says is (roughly) the meaning of what Sam said (namely, that there is a fire in the kitchen). The illocutionary force of Sam's utterance is the linguistic action that Sam performs in saying what he said. Sam is here telling Gavin (that there is a fire in the kitchen). Our focus now, however, is on the third kind of force: the perlocutionary force. The perlocutionary force of an utterance is the causal effect that the utterance has on its audience. In this case, Sam's utterance changes Gavin's beliefs. Sam's utterance causes Gavin to believe that there is a fire in the kitchen.

In this chapter, we are interested in utterances being prevented from having the impact that they ought to have. Rae Langton identified this phenomenon and called it 'perlocutionary frustration'; I will call it 'impact silencing'.[15] Impact silencing occurs when a speech action is prevented from impacting the world in certain ways that it should.

This notion of impact requires some clarification. There is a difference between the standard impact of a type of speech action and the impact that a particular speaker intends to bring about on any particular occasion. To see this difference in action, it's once again useful to consider some examples.

Looking Smart: Steve is a first year graduate student in philosophy and, over lunch during their first week, Steve tells his peers that simple and intuitive diagonalization arguments are used to prove (Godel's) incompleteness theorem. Steve doesn't really care whether anyone believes him; his primary aim is to look smart. Steve wants to set himself up as the leader of their cohort so that he can influence group dynamics for the better.

Covering One's Rear: Shirley is the safety manager for a school district and she orders the principals of each of the four schools in her district to instruct their students to use the crosswalks in the school parking lots. Shirley doesn't actually think the students will comply and she really doesn't care much whether the principals even follow through on her order; she just wants to go on record as having implemented this requirement in order to protect herself from any sort of liability in the extremely unlikely event that a student is hit by a vehicle in a school parking lot.

Signaling Character Traits: At a wedding, Dave apologizes to Mary for mistreating her some forty years ago. Dave's primary reason for doing so is to show his current girlfriend, Lana, what a sensitive, courageous, and principled guy he really is. Dave wants Lana to know that she can trust him. And, she can. Dave is a sensitive, courageous, and principled guy.

In each of these cases, the speaker's primary aim in performing their speech action departs from the standard aim for that kind of speech action. In *Looking Smart*, for example, Steve's primary aim is to be perceived as smart and to position himself as a leader even though the standard effect of telling people things is to get those people to believe those things. Similarly, in *Covering One's Rear*. The standard aim in issuing an order is to get others to follow that order but that was not Shirley's aim; Shirley aimed to protect herself from liability. Finally, in *Signaling Character Traits*, Dave apologizes to Mary in order to show Lana what sort of person he is; although Dave is apologizing to Mary, Dave is not aiming to repair his relationship with Mary; he aims instead to strengthen his relationship with Lana.

As one can see from these examples, the standard impact of a type of speech act can depart from what an individual speaker principally aims to do with that kind of speech act on a particular occasion. When writing about perlocution, though, Austin tended to talk about the perlocutionary effect of types of speech acts; in short, Austin was concerned with standard impacts. In thinking about impact prevention, though, we are right to be concerned with both standard impact and intended impact. For, if a speech act is prevented from having its standard effect, then that's a potential problem. But, it's also a potential problem if a speaker's words are prevented from having the effect that that speaker primarily intends.

Notice also that when we talk about impact prevention, we are concerned with the impact—whether standard or intended—that an utterance *ought to have*. So, another thing to keep in mind here is that we are implicitly making assumptions about how things *should* be. This normativity is unavoidable; it's also sometimes unavoidably controversial, and so it's best to have it out in the open.

> *Unheeded Warning*: Carl warns Sally that there is an accident on the route that Sally normally takes to work. Knowing that Carl got this "information" from his brother (who just makes stuff up willy nilly), Sally pretty much dismisses Carl's warning.

> *Unpersuasive Flat Earther*: John believes that the earth is flat and that all reports otherwise are unreliable. In attempting to convince Jane of this, he manages only to convince her that he is not a reliable source of scientific information.

In these cases, the speaker's intended impact (which is also the standard impact) is prevented. In *Unheeded Warning*, Carl aims to cause Sally to believe that there is an accident and to adjust her route accordingly. Carl's intended impact does not obtain. Sally does not trust him as a source of information, and so she does not update either her beliefs or her plans for driving to work. Similarly, in *Unpersuasive Flat Earther*, John aims to convince Jane that the earth is flat but he fails to do so. His intended impact is prevented.

Now, in these cases, we are probably ok with the results. That is, one might think that Sally's adjusting her route is not an impact that Carl's warning *ought* to have. So, too, with John's assertions. In light of his scientifically refuted world view, for instance, it seems sensible to think that his claims *should not* have the impact that he wants them to have (and that assertions typically have). If that's right, then these are not cases of impact prevention, as I have characterized it; impact prevention, as I have characterized it, requires that an utterance is prevented from having the impact that it *ought to* have. Since these utterances should not have their intended/standard impact, these are not cases of impact prevention.

Other cases, however, involve considerably more controversial judgments about what impact an utterance ought to have. To see this, let's look at some more cases.

> *Order Ignored*: The Deputy Chief orders his detective to stop investigating a murder case; for a variety of complicated reasons, some good and some quite bad, the detective ignores him. That detective also eventually gets results.

> *Unsuccessful Apology*: a wife sincerely apologizes to her husband of thirty years for something she did that was very wrong; her apology acknowledges her wrongdoing; she expresses a sincere intention to do better going forward; her apology is humbly offered and heartfelt, and she is rippled with regret. In short, it's a perfect apology. Despite this, her husband cannot let go of the resentment and, as much as he appreciates the apology, it does little to repair their relationship.[16]

In each of these cases, an utterance fails to have either its intended or its standard impact. The Deputy Chief's order is not followed and the wife's apology fails to repair her marital relationship. In these cases, though, it is much harder to say what impact these utterances ought to have, really. Maybe the detective definitely should have followed orders. Maybe not. It would depend on the details of the case and, even once all those details were specified, reasonable people might well disagree. For this reason, it is genuinely unclear what impact the Deputy Chief's order ought to have. After all, the real world is messy, and it is messy in exactly this way. The same can be said for *Unsuccessful Apology*. Whether or not a person should accept an apology and what effect that apology should have on one's relationship are deeply personal matters. These examples show that judgments about what impact an utterance ought to have can be really tricky and controversial. I raise this so we can keep it in mind. We should always keep it in mind. That said, going forward, I will aim to choose examples that are (or that I take to be) less controversial.[17]

In sum, impact prevention, as we have characterized it, involves an utterance being prevented from having the effect in the world that it ought to have. As we have seen, impact prevention is distinct from the various sorts of recognition failures we explored in the last chapter. In the next section, we consider the million dollar question: namely, whether impact prevention is a kind of silencing.

§ 5.5 Is Impact Prevention a Kind of Silencing: Should We Care?

Recall that silencing requires communicative failure. That is the one necessary condition of silencing identified back in Chapter 3. This means that in order for impact prevention to satisfy our characterization of silencing, it must involve communicative failure. But, does it?

To investigate this question, let's look again at *Small Pox*. In that case, the speaker's communicative intentions are recognized. The Bostonians recognize what kind of speech act Onesimus is performing; they know that Onesimus is asserting things. These skeptical Bostonians also recognize *what* Onesimus is claiming; in other words, the content of Onesimus's assertion is correctly identified. They also recognize Onesimus's sincerity; these Bostonians do not think that Onesimus is being dishonest with his claims. On this way of understanding what is happening in this case then, Onesimus's assertions about the efficacy of inoculation are successfully communicated. And, if that is right, then there does not seem to be any communicative failure in this case. So, it seems *Small Pox* does not involve silencing.

This reasoning is perfectly sound. To those working with a strict conception of communicative failure, impact silencing is a misnomer. On this way of thinking, what goes wrong in *Small Pox* is something other than silencing. It's a problem alright but it's not silencing *per se* and it's not silencing exactly because Onesimus successfully communicates his claims.

Recall again from Chapter 3, however, that we identified *three* conceptions of communicative failure. Here, they are again to refresh your memory:

Communicative Failure: Strict Version: Communicative failure involves an addressee not properly recognizing some aspect of what a speaker is trying to communicate.

Communicative Failure: Impact Version: Communicative failure (also) involves the prevention of the impact that a communication ought to have.[18]

Communicative Failure: Prevention Version: Communicative failure (also) involves the prevention of a particular communication attempt.

Although *Small Pox* does not satisfy the *Strict Version*, it does satisfy the *Impact Version*. Exactly because Onesimus's claims about inoculation do not have the evidential impact that they ought to have, exactly because the skeptical Bostonians' belief states do not change in the way that they should change in light of what Onesimus asserts, Onesimus's speech action is prevented from having the impact that it ought to have. On an *Impact Version of Communicative Failure* then, a credibility deficit is a form of communication failure and thus a candidate form of silencing.[19]

Ok, so which of the three versions of communicative failure is the right one? We're not going to try to settle that question here but it's worth reminding the reader that the right way to define things really does—and indeed should—depend on the purposes at hand. So, depending on what one needs a definition of silencing for, any combination of them could be appropriate.

If one's focus is exclusively on communication in the strict meta-intentional sense that linguists and philosophers of language use, for example, then the *Strict Version* makes sense. If, however, one is also concerned with the effects that our words have on the world around us, then the *Impact Version* is warranted. And if one wants to be able to include cases where people are physically prevented from speaking or staying silent out of fear, then the *Prevention Version* makes sense. (These sorts of cases will be explored in the next chapter.)

In this book, I accept each of the three versions, including the *Impact Version*. Since one goal of this book is to acknowledge and explore various ways that speech can be undermined, it ought to include impact prevention. After all, when speech is prevented from doing what it is supposed to do, our communicative capacities are pretty seriously undermined and that's relevant for my purposes.

Another reason to include impact prevention is that sometimes the intended impact is the *entire reason* for saying anything at all! To see this, consider the following case.

Warning Dismissed: Sarah notices black ice on the sidewalk in front of a convenience store. When she sees her elderly father approaching the store, she warns him about the slippery conditions by saying, "Hey dad, it's very slippery in front of the store; there's ice and I almost fell so please be careful". Her father understands her warning but considers himself fully coordinated and chooses to ignore it; he approaches the store, falls, and breaks his hip; Sarah watches it all in horror.

In *Warning Dismissed*, Sarah's warning is recognized but not heeded. Although Sarah's father understands exactly what she is warning him about (that is, there are no recognition failures here), he nevertheless decides to ignore her. Arguably, in this case, Sarah's entire point in speaking up at all is to prevent her father from falling. To bring this out, imagine that an obtuse philosopher of language was to point out to Sarah that her warning fully succeeds as a communicative act. In that case, do you really think that Sarah would be comforted to hear this? It might actually make matters worse! From Sarah's point of view, the entire point of her utterance was to protect her father and any communication with him was a mere means to that end. Sometimes, at least, the impact is the primary point, and this affords an additional reason to work with the *Impact Version* of communicative failure.

In the next section, I explore a particularly upsetting kind of impact prevention: failure to respect sexual refusals. Readers who could do without a discussion of sexual assault should skip to § 5.7.

§ 5.6 Impact Silencing and Rape

[CONTENT WARNING: sexual assault]

Before we even get started, it is worth stressing that, in this section, I am exploring sexual assault through the lens of silencing. This means that I will focus on communication-related issues associated with sexual assault. By focusing on these communication issues, I am by no means suggesting that these are the only issues or even the most important ones.

The literature on silencing and sexual refusals has a bit of a history. It started when Catharine MacKinnon famously claimed that certain kinds of pornography silence women.[20] (For MacKinnon, 'pornography' is being used in a special technical sense so it does not include all sexually explicit material, just the kind that eroticizes hierarchy and the brutalization of women.) MacKinnon's claim was met with criticism, even incredulity; she was subsequently accused of hyperbole and downright confusion.[21] Theorists offered ways to make sense of MacKinnon's claim, arguing that her claim is not only coherent; it's even plausible.

Here is one way to make sense of MacKinnon's claims.[22] Exposure to certain kinds of pornography leads consumers to make the sorts of interpretive mistakes that we discussed in the last chapter. Rae Langton and Jennifer Hornsby, for example, drew particular attention to how pornography consumption might lead consumers to fail to recognize a woman's intention to refuse.[23] Since this kind of recognition failure would prevent the successful communication of that refusal, the woman is thereby silenced. And, since pornography consumption caused the recognition failure, pornography causes the silencing constituted by that recognition failure. And, this is one way that it could turn out to be true that pornography silences women.[24]

This kind of account faced criticisms and one of them is worth addressing here. Some have expressed the concern that by focusing on recognition failures and the associated issues with communication, Langton and Hornsby are treating rape as a mere misunderstanding.[25] And, that their account both trivializes the harm of rape and undermines the responsibility of rapists.[26] Whether this kind of objection is apt depends on exactly what these accounts of silencing are aiming to do. If they aim to explain why rape happens or if their purpose is to identify all—or even the most important—harms of rape, then these objections would be powerful indeed. As it stands, however, the theoretical purpose of these accounts of silencing is importantly different. These accounts of silencing aim instead to identify ways that communication can be undermined; they aim to pinpoint how pornography might undermine women's communicative capacities; they seek to identify further communication-related harms that obtain in addition to all of the other harms.

Although recognition failure silencing can certainly obtain in cases of sexual assault, it is really the failure to respect the refusal that leads to rape. This suggests that impact prevention silencing is key. To see this, let's look at an example. Be warned: it's upsetting.

> *Not Respecting Refusal:* Betsy and Bill have been dating for three months. After a lovely dinner out together, they sit down to watch a movie at Betsy's apartment. One thing leads to another; they are both aroused; Betsy tries to put a stop to things by saying "No, Bill. Not yet; I'm not ready." Although Bill recognizes her sincere refusal, Bill nevertheless ignores it and forces himself on her.

In *Not Respecting Refusal*, Betsy's refusal is recognized but ignored; in refusing, Betsy aims to put a stop to the sexual encounter but that encounter continues against her will. Thus, although Betsy's sincere refusal is successfully communicated to Bill, her refusal does not have the impact that it ought to have. Betsy is here impact silenced.

In thinking about this case through the lens of silencing, it makes sense to first reflect a little bit on the nature of refusals. What exactly are we doing when we refuse? On the standard way of understanding refusal, it denies permission.[27] So, when Betsy sexually refuses, she denies Bill permission to proceed. Her refusal renders it morally (and in this case legally) impermissible for him to continue. Refusals are also (what are sometimes called) authoritative speech acts. This means that the speaker must have, and be exercising, a specific kind of authority.[28] In Betsy's case, she is exercising her authority over her own body. Betsy's primary aim in refusing is to stop Bill. When Bill proceeds anyway, he fails to respect Betsy's refusal. Her speech action of refusing does not have the (intended or standard) impact that it ought to have.

Notice that Betsy's refusal succeeds in a narrow communicative sense. In *Not Respecting Refusal*, Bill recognizes the various communicative components of Betsy's speech action of refusal. In particular, Bill realizes that Betsy is refusing; he recognizes that she is sincere in her refusal, and he recognizes that she has the authority to refuse. This is thus not a recognition failure sort of case. Instead, Betsy's refusal successfully gets through to Bill but he nevertheless fails to respect it; he goes ahead and does what he knows he is not permitted to do.

Our discussion so far has been pretty theoretical and even euphemistic. That's because this is a very upsetting sort of case but I will now lay it on the line: the impact silencing of sexual refusals plays a significant role in rape. No doubt there are sometimes recognition failures involved. A refusal might be mistaken for a different sort of speech act; it might be mistaken for mere role-playing, for encouragement, or even for consent. And, a sincere refusal might be mistaken for an insincere one. I do not mean to downplay the potential role of such recognition failure silencing. I just want to stress that impact silencing is a very large part of sexual assault. After all, many, probably most, perpetrators know full well that the victim has refused (or at least not consented) and proceed anyway.[29] There is no miscommunication; the victim's will has been knowingly violated.[30] As disturbing as this is, I leave the explanation for why it happens—and why it happens so often—to the social scientists.[31] As it stands, the impact silencing of sexual refusals is a widespread and profoundly harmful phenomenon.[32]

§ 5.7 Conclusion

In this chapter, I have shown how various speech acts can be impact silenced; they can be prevented from having the impact that they ought to have. I have also distinguished impact silencing from the sort of silencing I explored in Chapter 4, the sort that involves recognition failures during an attempted communication. In the next chapter, I look at yet another broad category of silencing. This time, I look at cases where an attempt to communicate is prevented altogether so either the speaker does not say what they otherwise would or they say nothing at all.

In closing, I will leave you with this quote that draws our attention to the impact of impact silencing:

> We live in a culture that ignores many voices. Insight, experience, and viewpoints are lost. The voices we do not hear often belong to people who are minority, female, and old. There are stories waiting to be told, and wisdom ready to be shared. When we laugh, cry, listen, and learn from others, the divisions between us begin to disappear.[33]

6

Not Saying That On Preventing Communication

I have already identified two different broad categories of silencing. One such type involves recognition failure during communication attempts. Another broad type of silencing involves impact prevention. In this chapter, we identify a third broad category of silencing: ways that attempts to communicate can be altogether prevented.[1]

So, it's not a case of miscommunication or a communication not achieving a certain effect, it's a case of preventing saying it at all.[2]

Let's look at some cases.

Malevolent SPED Teacher: Impatient with the constant verbalization of his anxious ADHD student, a misguided and callous special education teacher places duct tape on the student's mouth so that he can focus on the other students in the inclusive classroom.

Courtroom: After an outburst following the reading of a controversial verdict, a judge declares, "Silence in the courtroom!". Immediately, everyone in the courtroom stops speaking.

Authoritarian State: In a certain authoritarian regime, there is no explicit law prohibiting criticism of the regime but it is nevertheless well known that anyone even accused of criticizing the government can be jailed or even executed. Dissidents are therefore very careful in what they say and to whom.

On Silencing. Mary Kate McGowan, Oxford University Press. © Mary Kate McGowan 2026.
DOI: 10.1093/9780197837320.003.0006

Several points are worth making about these cases. First, each such case involves some particular speech action being prevented from taking place. In *Malevolent SPED Teacher*, the student is prevented from making any sounds at all; in *Courtroom*, the people in the court are prevented from speaking, and in *Authoritarian State*, the dissidents' criticisms are forestalled.

Second, their status as candidate cases of silencing is somewhat controversial. Intuitively, these cases seem like cases of silencing. The duct tape, the judge's order, and the authoritarian regime each seem to silence potential speakers. But, it is not clear that they satisfy the one necessary condition of silencing: communicative failure.

Here is one sensible way of thinking through this. One might think that failing to do something presupposes attempting to do that thing. As a result, one cannot fail unless one attempts. And, if that's right, communicative acts that are not even attempted would not count as failures. On this line of thinking then, the above cases are not cases of communication failure, and thus they are not potential instances of silencing.

These cases also do not satisfy our *strict version* of communicative failure. Recall that that conception requires an addressee failing to recognize some aspect of an attempted communication. Clearly, that's not happening here. There are no recognition failures in these cases exactly because the communicative acts in question are not even attempted. So, if one is strict about communicative failure, these cases do not count.

I am less strict and I am less strict for good reason. After all, we care about these sorts of cases and we're right to care. For this reason, I here rely on *Communicative Failure: Prevention Version* which treats communication prevention as a form of communicative failure. And, according to this version of communicative failure, the above cases count and are thus candidate cases of silencing.[3]

Third, the communication prevention in each of these cases is brought about by a different sort of mechanism. In *Malevolent SPED Teacher*, for example, the student is *physically* prevented from saying anything. In *Courtroom*, by contrast, it is *prescriptive*; it involves the enacting of obligations. The judge's declaration essentially orders those present to stop speaking. Finally, in *Authoritarian State*, justified fears about the consequences of speaking one's mind prevent people from doing so. As this case illustrates, a person can decide against speaking—not because they are physically prevented from speaking and not because they are ordered to remain silent—but because they want to avoid the anticipated consequences of speaking.

Fourth, although we might expect that silencing is always a bad thing or that it involves something being amiss, this does not seem to be the case in *Courtroom*. After all, judges do—and indeed should—have the authority to control what happens in their courtroom. The goal of deciding cases according to law requires all sorts of restrictions on who can say what and when in a court of law. And, while we might disagree with some of the rules, we have to admit that at least some rules are required. This suggests that at least sometimes silencing—at least as I have defined it—is what should happen, so not all instances of silencing are a bad thing.

If, however, one thinks that silencing has to be harmful, or group-based, or wrongful (to be of any theoretical interest), then one would add some additional necessary conditions to one's characterization of silencing and thus (potentially) disqualify what happens in *Courtroom* as an instance of it. Again, the right way to define something does—and indeed should—depend on one's interests.

So far, I have identified three different sorts of causes of communication attempt prevention. One can be physically prevented from saying something, as in *Malevolent SPED Teacher*; one can be prescriptively prevented from saying something, as in *Courtroom*, and one can decide against saying something because one wants to avoid the anticipated consequences of doing so, as in *Authoritarian State*. I am going to focus on the third kind of case—that is, deciding against speaking in order to avoid negative consequences—but before I do that, I first explore a bit of a complication.

The way I have so far described it, *Courtroom* is prescriptive; the judge ordered silence in the courtroom; the judge's utterance obligates those present to be silent. And, they are silent because they are following orders; they are adhering to the judge's prescription. Now, there is a sense in which those present in the courtroom are also *deciding against* speaking; in particular, they decide not to speak in order to avoid the negative consequences they know will result if they do speak, that is, if they do disobey the judge's order. So, seen in this way, *Courtroom* starts to look a lot like *Authoritarian State* (a decision against speaking in order to avoid the results).

And, *Authoritarian State* can also look a lot like *Courtroom*. Even though the dissidents decide against speaking in order to avoid the negative results of doing so, one might well take them to be adhering to implicit orders from the authoritarian state. After all, if severe state punishment reliably follows from saying certain sorts of things, then one could certainly make a case that saying those things is effectively prohibited by the state. Looking at it this way then, *Authoritarian State* seems prescriptive, much like *Courtroom*.

These considerations suggest that the difference between a prescription-following sort of case and a decision-to-avoid-negative-consequences sort of case can be blurry. It also shows that some prescriptions are implicit. In other words, not all normative expectations are explicitly spelled out or backed up by official sorts of power. Think, for example, of social norms prohibiting public nose picking. We are expected to refrain from doing this but it's not a law or a moral requirement and it's not written down anywhere or sanctioned in any official way. OK, so things are messy. What to do about this?

In what follows, I am going to focus on cases of deciding against speaking. In doing so, I will leave it open whether such cases are also helpfully understood as cases of following (implicit) norms. I am therefore leaving behind cases where a person is physically prevented from speaking and cases where an explicit order prevents one from doing so. Although these cases are interesting and certainly worthy of our collective attention, as we shall soon see, I have plenty to discuss in focusing as narrowly as I am.

One more clarification before I really get started. There is a difference between deciding against saying a certain thing (and maybe saying something else instead) and deciding against speaking at all. Let's see this with two versions of *Authoritarian State.*

Authoritarian State: Say Nothing: Jim is a citizen in an authoritarian state where anyone so much as accused of criticizing the government can be jailed or even executed. Although Jim deeply disagrees with the policies of the state, Jim decides to say nothing at all about the regime.

Authoritarian State: Toe The Line: Jaylan is a citizen in an authoritarian state where anyone so much as accused of criticizing the government can be jailed or even executed. Although Jaylan deeply disagrees with the state's policies, Jaylan decides to praise the regime instead of voicing her genuine beliefs.

As one can see, one can decide against saying a particular thing and say something else instead—as Jaylan does in *Authoritarian State: Toe The Line*—or one can say nothing at all—as Jim does in *Authoritarian State: Say Nothing*. Strictly speaking, I am interested in both sorts of cases. That said, sometimes, and primarily for the sake of simplicity, I talk as if both cases are cases of saying nothing. When it comes to voicing their criticisms of the authoritarian state, both Jim and Jaylan decide against it. So, although Jaylan chooses to say something else instead, she is silent with respect to her criticisms. Going forward then, I will not continue to stress this difference.

§ 6.1 Decisions Against Speaking: Self-Silencing

Notice first that there are all sorts of reasons why a person might decide against saying a certain thing. A person might remain silent because it is someone else's turn to speak, because one has nothing relevant—or sufficiently supported—to say, or just because one is tired. But, these sorts of reasons for not speaking are importantly different from those operative in *Authoritarian State*. There, the dissidents refrain from speaking in order to avoid unjust punishments that are genuinely harmful.

In what follows, I narrow my focus significantly; I henceforth focus on what I am calling 'harm avoidance self-silencing'. When a speaker decides against saying a certain thing and she does so in order to *avoid the anticipated harms* of doing so, we have harm-avoidance self-silencing. *Authoritarian State* involves a canonical example of harm-avoidance self-silencing.[4] By narrowing my focus in this way, I am in no way claiming that other sorts of reasons against speaking do not involve silencing. Rather, I remain agnostic about all other cases. I focus as I do because harm-avoidance self-silencing is an important phenomenon and I need to make the discussion manageable.

As we shall see, what counts as harm-avoidance self-silencing can depend on what counts as harm. Although there are robust philosophical controversies regarding this, I am not here offering (or even relying on) any such an account. Instead, I rely on common sense conceptions of what is harmful.

Let's get started with a case.

Unionization: Tom has a one-year post-doctoral fellowship at a university where the non-tenure-track faculty recently unionized. Under pressure, Tom reluctantly joined the union but is against the potential strike being discussed by several of his non-tenure track colleagues in the faculty lounge. Tom believes that it is professionally irresponsible for primary instructors to strike during term time and he also believes that the union's current salary demands are unreasonable. Sensing that the others would not react well to the expression of his views, Tom decides to keep them to himself.[5]

In *Unionization*, Tom decides against speaking but it is not because he isn't a part of the conversation; he is welcome to join in. And, it's not because he has nothing relevant or sufficiently supported to say; Tom has given this a lot of thought; he has discussed it with colleagues at other institutions, and he has even done some market research on faculty compensation. No, the reason Tom decides to remain silent is because he wants to avoid experiencing the reaction of his audience if he were to say what he actually thinks.

Is this a case of anticipated harm self-silencing? Well, unsurprisingly, it depends. And, it depends on what the reaction would be and what Tom knows or believes about what that reaction would be. To make this more concrete, let's consider another version of the case with some of these consequences spelled out more fully.

§ 6.1.1 Mere Disagreement

Unionization: Mere Disagreement: The situation is the same as in *Unionization* but in this case, Tom decides against voicing his opinion because he knows that the other faculty members in the lounge will disagree with him; Tom is tired and stressed and he knows that he needs to pick his battles, so he decides to say nothing.

Is this a case of harm-avoidance self-silencing? In other words, did Tom decide against speaking in order to avoid harms that would result if he did?

On the surface anyway, it doesn't seem to be. Typically, a person isn't harmed when others disagree with them. So, Tom's decision to refrain from saying what he otherwise would say does not seem to be based on his desire to avoid harmful consequences. If that's correct, then it's not a potential case of harm-avoidance self-silencing.

That said, even if Tom's *reasons for* refraining from speaking do not involve harm avoidance, that doesn't mean that this case is harmless. There could well be harms involved here. Suppose, for example, that many other faculty members feel the way Tom does but they all remain silent because they falsely believe that they are outnumbered; the ensuing strike harms the most vulnerable students, tears the faculty apart, and leads to a public relations nightmare that so crushes the university's finances that it is forced to close. If this is what happens, then Tom's decision against speaking *contributes* to causal processes that are harmful.

Even so, that is not enough to make it an instance of harm-avoidance self-silencing, at least as I have defined it. Since Tom here decides against speaking in order to avoid disagreement and since being disagreed with isn't harmful, *Unionization: Disagreement Version* isn't an instance of harm-avoidance self-silencing.

At this point, it is worth flagging a potential nuance. Although being disagreed with isn't *typically* harmful, in certain kinds of cases, it might be. To see this sort of possibility, consider the following.

> *Rejecting Racism*: Sally, a woman of color, experiences yet another racist event at work. Although she feels compelled to point it out, she knows that her (mostly white) co-workers will disagree with her yet again. Exhausted by the never-ending task of trying to educate her white work colleagues, Sally decides against saying anything this time.[6]

In *Rejecting Racism*, Sally decides against speaking because she just does not have the energy to engage with the inevitable resistance, denial, and disagreement that would ensue. All too often, the work of fighting racism falls disproportionately on those already harmed by it. Both racism and the burden of fighting it are harmful. Seen in this light, one might well regard the anticipated disagreement in *Resisting Racism* as harmful. And, if it is, then Sally's decision to refrain from speaking is a potential instance of harm-avoidance self-silencing.[7]

§ 6.1.2 Harm Avoidance

Let's now consider other sorts of audience reactions that might ensue from Tom expressing his opinion in that faculty lounge. Lots of reactions are possible. To fix ideas, we'll consider another version of the case.

> *Unionization: Social Punishment*: Tom's non-tenure-track colleagues are very angry at the university and at anyone who does not wholeheartedly and unquestionably support their cause. Were Tom to so much as question the legitimacy of a strike, Tom would be vilified. He would be maligned, harassed, and socially shunned by his non-tenure-track colleagues; he would also be cancelled by most of the students. Since Tom really needs high enrollments and stellar evaluations to get a permanent job in academia somewhere else (after his one year contract at this institution ends), he decides to keep his opinions to himself.

Now, if this is why Tom decides to remain silent, it's a different story. Arguably, it's a very different story. There is much to say here, but we will focus on the possibility that Tom decides against speaking in order to avoid harms that he reasonably believes would result from him speaking his mind. Looking at the case this way, *Unionization: Social Punishment* looks quite a bit like *Authoritarian*

State, where dissidents refrain from expressing criticism of the regime in order to avoid an unjust and harmful punishment.

In what follows, I identify potential sorts of harms that Tom believes would result from him speaking and the avoidance of which leads to his decision to remain silent. The first potential kind of harm is fairly obvious; it concerns the various consequences of Tom being socially punished for expressing unpopular views. In particular, Tom anticipates being maligned and harassed; he also expects that the students will not take his classes and give him bad evaluations even if they do. Were this to happen, it could well destroy any chance he has of ever getting a permanent position in his field. And, if Tom remains silent to avoid these harms, then it seems to be an instance of harm-avoidance self-silencing.[8]

There are additional potential harms that are less obvious. For starters, there is the possibility of damaged credibility. As we saw in Chapter 5, a credibility deficit (that is, not being given the credibility that one ought to be given) is a kind of impact prevention; it's a kind of silencing. And, in *Unionization: Social Punishment*, Tom might well decide to say nothing because he believes that what he has to say will be met with more skepticism than is warranted. In other words, Tom will be given less credibility than he deserves, and this happens exactly because he is outnumbered and his audience is angry. So, even if some of his audience will understand perfectly well what he is saying (and what he means in saying it so there are no recognition failures), Tom realizes that his colleagues are nevertheless seriously disinclined to give what he says its proper weight. In addition to the possibility of having his conversational contribution devalued in this particular context, Tom might be concerned about longer-term credibility deflation. That is, once he is recognized as an enemy to the cause, that status could well lead to future claims of Tom's being devalued. So, if Tom chooses to remain silent here in order to avoid either immediate or longer-term credibility deflation and if credibility deficits are harmful, then this is another way that Tom's decision to keep it to himself could be an instance of harm-avoidance self-silencing.

Anticipated recognition failures are another potential harm, Tom might be concerned that his speaker meaning will be misunderstood, his sincerity questioned, or his motivations for speaking misidentified. And, if any of these sorts of recognition failures are harmful, then this is yet another way in which Tom is here potentially harm-avoidance self-silencing.

I have here identified three different potential harms whose antic-ipation could give rise to Tom's decision to remain silent. Although I have taken care to separate these distinct potential harms and consequent forms of harm-avoidance self-silencing, they could all be happening together in *Unionization: Social Punishment.*

§ 6.1.3 On the Anticipation of Harm

Before moving on to consider additional forms of self-silencing, it makes sense to slow down and think more thoroughly through a speaker's decision against speaking in order to avoid the anticipated harms of doing so. There are some subtle (and even controversial) questions here: Must the speaker be correct about the harms that would ensue? Must the speaker have a true and justified belief that these harms would result? That is, must the speaker *know* that the harms would result? Are there any cases where the speaker is wrong but their belief about the harms is nevertheless justified and there-fore reasonable?

Let's dig in and see where it lands us. Once again, I will consider a series of cases.

Warranted True Belief: Sarah believes her workplace is unenlight-ened about gender injustice. In particular, she believes that if she reports incidents of sexual harassment, she would be dismissed, blamed, and professionally punished for doing so. As a result, she decides against reporting any of it. As it turns out, Sarah is absolutely correct to believe this; she also has ample evidence given what has happened to other women over the years.

In *Warranted True Belief,* Sarah decides against speaking in order to avoid being punished for doing so. And, in her case, her beliefs about what would happen are both true and well supported. This seems to be an uncontroversial case of harm-avoidance self-silencing. Sarah decides against saying what she would otherwise say in order to avoid the unjust harms that she knows would result if she said it.

Things get a bit more interesting—and more controversial, though—when we change things up a bit. Here is another case.

Warranted but False Belief: Sarah believes her workplace is un-enlightened about gender injustice. In particular she believes that if she reported incidents of sexual harassment, she would be dismissed, blamed, and professionally punished for doing so. As a result, she decides against reporting any of it. As it turns out, Sarah is wrong. Although she has ample evidence given what has happened to other women over the years at this firm, her colleagues have since seen the light. An especially effective documentary streaming on Netflix – which they all happened to watch – has sufficiently sensitized them to the relevant issues.

Sarah decides against speaking here because she has a well-supported and thus reasonable belief that harm will result if she does speak up. But, in this case, Sarah is wrong. What to say in a case like this one?

There are certainly considerations in favor of taking this to be a potential and even troubling instance of harm-avoidance self-silencing even though Sarah's belief is false. For starters, Sarah's evidence in *Warranted but False Belief* is exactly the same as it is in *Warranted True Belief.* This suggests that we might want to treat the two cases alike. After all, since Sarah's evidence is the same, so too, it seems are the social pressures inhibiting her expression. Cases like this are also one reason why Kristie Dotson suggests that audience members have a responsibility to signal their awareness to potential speakers.[9] On this line of thinking, Sarah's newly enlightened co-workers should somehow let her know that they are now more aware of gender issues. And, one reason they should do this is to prevent her from harm-avoidance self-silencing.

So much for reasonable false beliefs. What should we say about unreasonable ones? We certainly could say that anytime a person decides against speaking in order to avoid harms that that person thinks would result is a case of harm-avoidance self-silencing. This is a very broad conception of self-silencing, and it is an option. That said, going forward, I will restrict my attention to cases of reasonable belief. This is a sensible decision but it's important to stress that what is reasonable can be contested.[10] Reasonable people can, and indeed do, disagree about what's reasonable!

§ 6.2 Dotson's Testimonial Smothering

Kristie Dotson has given a name to, and an account for, an important form of harm-avoidance self-silencing; she calls it 'testimonial smothering'.[11] In naming this phenomenon, Dotson is drawing attention to work in Black feminism that has been overlooked. It should be no surprise that women of color have been theorizing about various silencing phenomena for ages; it's lived experience; it's just that that work has not been properly recognized by others in the academy. Before considering Dotson's analysis, let's look at one of our original motivating examples.

No Police Report: Linda is an African American woman who experiences domestic abuse. She decides against reporting it to the police because she fears that the only result of doing so would be to reinforce the stereotype, already present in the minds of the police and society at large, that Black men are violent.[12]

Let's first get clear on what exactly concerns Linda. In *No Police Report,* Linda is not concerned, as many victims of domestic abuse are, that she will not be believed. On the contrary, Linda thinks that the police might be a bit too disposed to believe her. And, Linda is not concerned that the police will somehow misunderstand what she is saying or what she is aiming to do with her words.

Instead, Linda believes that the police will over-generalize, that is, they will take her testimony as better evidence than it actually is and use it to support a false generalization about Black men. In short, Linda is concerned that because the police are affected by stereotypes about Black men, they will reason in a faulty way with the evidence that she would otherwise provide. And, in order to avoid a pernicious stereotype from being reinforced, Linda decides against reporting the abuse.

Dotson calls this 'testimonial smothering'. Testimonial smothering occurs when a speaker truncates their testimony (that is, removes some specific content) because the speaker realizes that the audience is not competent to receive what they have to say and harm will result from this incompetence. *Domestic Abuse* is a clear instance. Linda does not report the abuse (that is, she truncates her testimony) because she realizes that the police are affected by stereotypes about Black men and are thus incompetent to reason properly with her (potential) report. The police's improper reasoning would be harmful because it would reinforce a harmful stereotype about Black men.

Dotson stresses that testimonial smothering depends on several factors. First, it's relative to content. While Linda might decide against telling the police about the domestic abuse, she might not hesitate to report a car accident. Testimonial smothering is relative in this way because audience competence is also relative to content. In other words, while police officers in the throes of racist stereotypes are not competent to receive testimony about violent Black husbands, they are competent to receive other sorts of testimony. Second, smothering is also relative to audience. While Linda might decide against telling the police about the abuse, she might very well share her experience with her close friends, who *are* competent to receive her testimony. Third and finally, smothering is sensitive to a context. On a different occasion, in a different state of mind or with different signals coming from the officers, Linda might decide to tell the police about the abuse. As one can see, testimonial smothering is a highly relative phenomenon.

It's also a really useful one. After all, speakers routinely adjust what they have to say in order to avoid the anticipated costs of speaking. And, when those costs are unjust harms, it seems right to consider it a form of silencing.

It's worth stressing again that silencing itself can be one of the anticipated harms that lead to testimonial smothering. If, for example, a speaker believes that she will be misunderstood, then she might well decide against saying it; she might even decide against saying anything at all. If one knows that one's refusal will not be respected or one's assertion will not be believed, one might not issue them in the first place. Since the anticipation of silencing can lead to testimonial smothering, silencing begets silencing. Furthermore, when people self-silence, their voices are underrepresented, which can reinforce stereotypes that lead to further forms of silencing. These are just some of the ways—and there are many more—in which the different forms of silencing can interact and mutually reinforce one another.

As important as testimonial smothering is, in some ways, it's quite narrow. Recall that testimonial smothering depends on the content; in particular, it depends on the speaker's awareness of the audience's incompetence with respect to that content. This characterization of smothering is narrow because audiences can be incompetent about things other than content. To see this, consider the following cases.

> *New Bedford*: Jill has a heavy regional accent. While being interviewed for a position at a law firm in Weston, MA, she decides to hide her accent. She knows that those interviewing her will think less of her if she sounds like she is from New Bedford.

> *Stutter*: Joe has a stutter. Realizing that many people misunderstand his condition, he tends to say as little as possible when around people like that.

> *Dialect*: Sarah grew up in a community speaking (a form of) African American English. She knows that most white people falsely believe that Standard American English is the only correct way to speak American English, so, when Sarah is around white people, she adjusts what she says and how she says it.[13]

As these examples demonstrate, aspects of an utterance—other than its content—can trigger biases in the audience. And, a speaker's awareness of these biases can lead to harm-avoidance self-silencing. As many readers already know from their lived experience, some African American English (AAE) speakers take on the added burden of switching to Standard American English (SAE) (this is called 'code-switching') or blending aspects of AAE with SAE (which is called 'code-meshing'), as Sarah does in *Dialect*. Once again, we see that the burden of other people's ignorance falls on people who are already marginalized. Dotson herself is well aware of these phenomena but had independent reason to characterize testimonial smothering in terms of content. For our purposes, though, it makes sense to be aware of non-content based self-smothering.

§ 6.3 On Politeness and Harm-Avoidance
Self-Silencing

There are plenty of reasons (other than harm avoidance) why a speaker might decide against saying a particular thing. And, politeness considerations are one of them. This is familiar enough. To see this, consider the following.

> *Carbuncle*: Astrid has a huge zit at the tip of her nose. Her work colleague, Tim, decides against saying anything about it because he knows that it would be very rude for him to do so.

Here, Tim refrains from saying something in order to avoid being rude. This case seems perfectly commonplace. Moreover, it seems that counting as rude wouldn't be at all harmful to Tim. If that is correct, then *Carbuncle* is not a potential instance of harm-avoidance self-silencing. The politeness norms operative does not seem to interfere with Tim's ability to safely and successfully communicate.

It is important to realize, however, that politeness expectations are not born equally. Some people, typically people with less social power, are expected to be *more* polite. And, this is unfair. It restricts behavior; it signals (unwarranted) deference, and abiding by these unjust and heightened expectations can be exhausting.

To see what I have in mind here, consider how women are socially expected to smile in response to inappropriate comments about their appearance. Think about how people of color are expected to spend the extra energy to figure out a way to respond to racist comments that protects the feelings of those insensitive enough to say them in the first place. Sadly, many readers will already be all too familiar with this phenomenon. In what follows, I draw our attention to how this sort of thing can contribute to harm-avoidance self-silencing.

Once again, I will jump right in with some cases.

Alone in a Bar: Carmen is alone in a bar; she is having a glass of wine to decompress after a stressful week as a homicide detective. Several men approach her but, when she signals to them that she would prefer to be alone with her thoughts, they keep trying to convince her that their company is just what she needs.[14]

Reluctant Consent: Ava and Peter meet at a nightclub and are immediately attracted to one another. Back at his apartment, Ava is repulsed by his behavior but reluctantly consents to sex. She just does not have the emotional energy to try to figure out how to gracefully duck out of what she allowed to get this far.[15]

Not That Snowflake: Gem is a transwoman and she has just been deliberately misgendered by Irene, a work colleague. Irene has done this many times before; Irene pretends to be oblivious but Gem suspects that Irene actually gets a kick out of making Gem squirm, struggling with decisions about what, if anything, to do. Knowing that any attempt to hold Irene to task will count as Gem being both oversensitive and incredibly rude, Gem opts to say - and to do - nothing.

In each of these cases, a speaker decides against saying what they want to say, and they do so in order to avoid counting as really rude.[16] In *Alone in a Bar*, for example, Carmen wants to tell these men to leave her the hell alone but she knows that, if she does this, she will be perceived as completely out of line. And, she's just too exhausted right now to deal with this.

So, she tolerates unwanted company in order to avoid it. In *Reluctant Consent*, Ava decides against refusing an unwanted sexual encounter, and she does so because she doesn't currently have the energy to figure how to do so without being perceived as conniving and shitty. Finally, in *Not That Snowflake*, Gem doesn't object to humiliating mistreatment, and she does so precisely because she knows that she will be socially punished for raising any kind of fuss about it.

In short, stricter politeness expectations can be harmful. When they are and when speakers decide against speaking in order to avoid counting as rude, we have harm-avoidance self-silencing. Although politeness norms can certainly be socially beneficial; they coordinate behavior and signal respect, politeness norms, especially when elevated for less socially powerfully folks, can also be a site of injustice.

§ 6.4 Conclusion

In this chapter, I have investigated a third broad type of silencing involving the prevention of communication attempts. I have also shown that communication attempt prevention can be physical; it can be prescriptive, and it can involve a decision to avoid the anticipated harms of speaking. Focusing on this third type, harm-avoidance self-silencing, where a speaker decides against saying a particular thing in order to avoid anticipated harms, I also explored the sinister side of politeness.

In the next chapter, I change gears a bit and consider phenomena that contribute to each of the three broad kinds of silencing. These phenomena are not themselves forms of silencing but they do contribute—in foreseeable ways—to each of the three broad kinds thus far identified.

7

Some Complex Contributors

In this chapter, I shift away from the central question of this book (i.e., what is silencing?) to thinking about some of the things that cause it. It is one thing to give an account of silencing, that is, to say what it is and to identify the various forms that it can take. And, it is another thing to identify the things in the world that make silencing happen. Here, in this chapter, I will consider some of these contributors to silencing.[1]

For any particular instance of silencing, there will be many causes. Since any cause of a cause is also a cause, it would be futile to try to identify them all. There are just too many causes. One needs to be selective. In light of this, I have decided to focus on three phenomena; each of which causes each of the three broad types of silencing. For this reason, I call them 'complex contributors' to silencing.

In § 7.1, I explore how false beliefs about how to correctly speak American English cause all three types of silencing. Then, in § 7.2, I explore the shared conceptual resources in a linguistic community. There, I show how false beliefs about what is genuinely shared can lead to silencing in each of the three broad ways identified. Finally, in § 7.3, I look at how we (mis)read one another's emotions and how these mistakes can cause the various kinds of silencing, too.

By focusing on these three things in particular, I am in no way suggesting that these are the only complex contributors to silencing. Unfortunately for the prospect of a society free of silencing, there are many more such complex contributors. Let's get started with our first complex contributor: false beliefs about language.

On Silencing. Mary Kate McGowan, Oxford University Press. © Mary Kate McGowan 2026.
DOI: 10.1093/9780197837320.003.0007

§ 7.1 Dialects

Most Americans realize that the English language is spoken differently in different parts of the globe. Your average American citizen, for example, realizes that British people use different pronunciation patterns, have a different accent, and use different words. So too with the Irish, the Scottish, and the Australian. Although Americans realize that English varies across the globe, many Americans do not realize that it varies in the United States too. And, this variation is not just a matter of different (regional) accents.[2] There are many *dialects* of English spoken here in the United States, and, as we shall now see, widespread failures to recognize this leads to each of the three forms of silencing.

To fix ideas, I will focus on two such dialects: Standard American English (SAE) and African American English (AAE). Now, the names of these dialects are each controversial. SAE is sometimes called Academic English (AE), Mainstream American English (MAE), and Standard Edited American English (SEAE). AAE is also sometimes called African American Vernacular English (AAVE), Ebonics, U.S. Ebonics, Black English (BE) or African American Language (AAL).[3] Very roughly, SAE is the kind of English spoken in schools, the criminal justice system, and the media. AAE is the kind of English spoken in (some) Black communities.

As linguists have been stressing for years, AAE is a genuine dialect, with its own grammar, vocabulary, and rules of pronunciation. Although AAE is a distinct dialect, linguistically on a par with SAE, it is nevertheless often mistaken for "bad English".[4] The widespread, but false, belief that SAE is the only correct way to speak (American) English leads to a variety of further mistakes and injustices; linguist Rosina Lippi-Green calls this 'language subordination'.[5] And, as we shall now see, silencing is among the injustices caused.[6]

No doubt many readers are already well aware of this. No doubt, those same readers are well aware of how many remain unaware.

Although I cannot do justice to all of the issues involved, I can and will highlight how this lack of awareness silences. Let's jump right in with a case.

> *Meta-ignorance*: Betty is being questioned in a court of law and the following exchange takes place.

> LAWYER: Is John married?
> BETTY: Yes. He bin married.

Members of the jury interpret Betty's utterance of 'bin' to be an incorrect shorthand for 'has been'. In short, they interpret her as meaning that John has been but is not currently married. In interpreting her this way, jurors are confused by Betty's saying 'yes' to the question. In light of this, they take her to have contradicted herself. Understanding themselves as generous and charitable, they infer that Betty must have misunderstood the question somehow. Despite their self-presumed generosity in interpreting Betty, jurors take her to be neither well educated nor bright.[7]

In AAE, there are more forms of the verb 'to be' than in SAE.[8] One such form is 'bin'. Translating 'bin' into SAE, it means something like 'is and has been for quite some time'. So, when Betty said, 'he bin married', Betty expressed the claim that John is currently married and he has been married for a long time now. Although that is what she said, jurors took her to mean something else; they took her to mean that he was but is no longer married. Notice that this is no subtle mistake; the misunderstood content actually contradicts the actual content. Moreover, Betty's utterance is neither ungrammatical nor contradictory. The juror's false belief that Betty must be speaking SAE, grounded in their false belief that SAE is the only way to perform English in the United States, leads jurors to make these mistakes. And, as we shall now see, these mistakes lead to each of the three broad types of silencing.

First, jurors misunderstand the content of what Betty is actually saying. Their ignorance of AAE leads them to misinterpret the conventional meaning of the words uttered; in short, Betty's statement is misunderstood; she fails to communicate the content that she intends to get across; this is a case of communicative interference resulting from a recognition failure. Betty is here content silenced.

Second, Betty is also impact silenced. By taking her to be uneducated, not very smart, and contradicting herself, jurors do not give her testimony the credibility it deserves. As one can see, it is the juror's false belief that Betty must be speaking (or trying to speak) SAE that is leading them to infer these false negative things about her.[9] Jurors mistake Betty's perfectly grammatical claim in AAE for an ungrammatical claim in SAE. And, from their false belief that she has been ungrammatical, jurors take her to be uneducated. Also, by misunderstanding the meaning of what she said, jurors mistakenly take Betty to have contradicted herself. And, all of these things lead jurors to underestimate Betty's credibility as a witness. Betty's words do not have the effect in the world that she intends them to have and that they ought to have. Consequently, Betty is here impact silenced.

Notice how these two forms of silencing result from the ignorance of the jurors. Oh the irony that Betty is mistakenly taken to be ignorant as a direct result of the jurors' ignorance. For many readers, this pattern is a very familiar one. When someone doesn't know what they don't know, they are ignorant of their own ignorance. As we saw in Chapter 4, this is called meta-ignorance; hence the name for the case.[10]

Third, AAE speakers' awareness of this widespread meta-ignorance can certainly lead to harm-avoidance self-silencing. In some contexts, AAE speakers might well decide to say nothing at all when they anticipate being misunderstood or read as ignorant, uneducated, or misinformed. AAE speakers also adjust what they say and how they say it. As we saw in the previous chapter, in anticipation of such consequences, some AAE speakers code-switch or code-mesh. Plainly, there is an unjust imbalance here. AAE speakers are required to speak SAE (in public schools, the criminal justice system, and many employment contexts) but SAE speakers are able to remain blissfully ignorant of even the existence of AAE, never mind learn to speak or properly understand it.[11] This too is a widespread pattern where marginalized persons must do extra work to navigate the social world shaped by the meta-ignorance of others.[12]

Unrecognized dialectical differences in the United States lead to all three forms of silencing. And, those harmed by this are those already marginalized. The widespread but false belief that SAE is the only correct way to speak American English is thus a complex contributor to silencing. In the next section, I explore another.

§ 7.2 Conceptual Impoverishment

Conceptual impoverishment is another complex contributor to silencing; it causes all three kinds.[13] But, before I explore the many ways that conceptual impoverishment leads to silencing, I must first explain what conceptual impoverishment is.

When we communicate, we rely on a shared understanding of the meaning of the words that we use. When Catherine says to Sam, "the train is late", for example, Sam is able to understand what Catherine aims to tell him in large part because Sam knows what those words mean. And, Sam also knows that Catherine knows what they mean and she knows that he knows and so on. The meaning of what Catherine said is something that Sam and Catherine share. And, when we use words to communicate, we very much—and quite obviously—rely on this shared understanding of the conventional meaning of the words we use.

We also rely on shared understanding of the *social* meaning of words and of the things they refer to. Let's see this sort of thing in action.

Really Not Your Type: Jim is interested in asking Jane on a date so he asks a mutual friend, Sarah, whether he should proceed. Sarah offers a knowing smile and says, "Well, Jim, you've managed to miss a cue or two; Jane is definitely not your type; she might as well drive a Subaru." Jim gets the point and wonders what other signs he might have missed.

Here, Sarah successfully communicates to Jim that Jane is a lesbian; Jim recognizes Sarah's speaker meaning because he knows the social meaning of Subaru ownership. If Jim did not know that Subaru ownership is associated with lesbianism, he would not have recognized what Sarah aimed to tell him. And, Sarah relied on Jim knowing this. Otherwise, she should have chosen another way to convey what she meant. In this way, we see that a shared understanding of social meaning is also crucial to successful communication.

A problem arises, however, when the available shared meanings—either linguistic or social—do not reflect (or do not make it easy to express) what a speaker aims to get across. When this happens, it is at least more difficult (if not impossible) for that person to successfully communicate.

Feminist philosophers of language have long been concerned with ways in which social power and group membership affect the shared conceptual resources of a linguistic community. As they have argued, the shared meaning of terms tends not to reflect the experiences of women.[14] Furthermore, this is so, even when the term in question concerns women! Consider, as an example of this, the social meaning of motherhood. Society tends to portray motherhood as a gift that fully fulfills a woman and puts her into an effortless and perpetual state of love. Idealizing motherhood in this way can interfere with women's ability to communicate about their inevitably non-ideal experiences of motherhood.[15] As feminist philosophers of language have long stressed, the meaning of terms and the concepts available in a language tend to represent the interests and experiences of those in power. If this is correct, then this means that actual languages are ill equipped to express and successfully communicate the experiences and interests of marginalized persons.[16]

Let's focus on an example. Before pioneering feminist legal work made the concept of hostile environment sexual harassment socially salient, women who experienced the phenomenon did not have the conceptual resources to communicate effectively about their harrowing workplace experiences.[17,18] Prior to these legal advances, sexual harassment in the workplace needed to take a 'sleep with me or you are fired' form. The idea that a work environment could be hostile to women (in a way that is discriminatory because it denies women equal access to the workplace) was neither socially nor legally recognized. A hostile workplace environment was a phenomenon alright (that is, it happened) but it was not recognized as such, and there was no linguistic expression for it.[19] As a result of this legal work and corresponding social changes, hostile environment is now "a thing"; it's thereby easier to recognize, discuss, and even remedy. The main point for now is that prior to these developments, a dearth of shared conceptual resources interfered with the ability to communicate about this kind of harassment.

To spell out the potential connections to silencing, let's consider an example.

Mad Men: Nora is a secretary in a New York advertising agency during the 1960s. Her male co-workers routinely comment on her body and appearance; they touch her in overly familiar ways without her consent, and they tell jokes that operate on the assumption that women are stupid and only good for one thing. Intending to object to this discriminatory treatment, Nora reports the harassment to her boss, Lance, when she says, "I'm not treated the way the men are; I have to deal with all those comments and unwanted touches and the men do not". Despite

Nora's best efforts, Lance just doesn't get it; he thinks she ought to stop wasting his time and just appreciate all the compliments.[20]

As we shall now see, Nora can be silenced in each of the three ways. First, there are recognition failures. For starters, Lance fails to realize that Nora is objecting; her illocutionary intention to object goes unrecognized. As far as Lance is concerned, this treatment is a compliment to Nora's attractiveness, and so there is really no legitimate problem here at all. And, while Lance instructs Nora to get back to work, he thinks to himself "Of course, you're treated differently; you're a broad, for God's sake! What did you expect?!" In short, Lance mistakes Nora's protest as misguided complaining; he also fails to recognize her intended meaning. Lance does not even realize that Nora is talking about discrimination. Not having a shared understanding of hostile workplace sexual harassment interferes with Nora's ability to communicate successfully with Lance about it; Nora is recognition failure silenced.

Second, Lance's misinterpretations will no doubt lead to impact silencing. Nora's protest will not have the impact that it ought to have; it will not, that is, lead to Lance taking steps to improve the workplace environment. Nora's words will be prevented from having the impact they ought to have; Nora is impact silenced.

In addition to this, Lance's misunderstanding of what Nora said will lead to further instances of Nora being impact silenced. Precisely because Lance takes Nora to have just complained about what he regards as perfectly normal behavior, Lance concludes that Nora is unreasonable, oversensitive, and misguided. As far as Lance is concerned, Nora should have appreciated the compliments—not expected to be treated like a man, which she is not. Confounded by Nora's claims, Lance takes them as good evidence that Nora is both confused and fragile and her perceptions are not to be trusted. As one can see then, Lance's interpretive mistakes lead him to lower his estimation of Nora's credibility. And, this will lead to further instances of Nora being impact silenced.

Third and finally, Nora's being aware of Lance's obtuseness can lead her to harm-avoidance self-silence. After what happens, she might well decide to keep her mouth shut about any of this in the future. After all, her attempt to raise awareness and to make the workplace culture better only managed to make things worse; she was misunderstood, maligned, and discredited. In light of all this then, one can well understand why Nora might not try again. Moreover, other employees, seeing how Nora fares, might well decide to curb what they have to say as well. All of these considerations show how conceptual impoverishment can cause harm-avoidance self-silencing.

As one can see then, conceptual impoverishment is a complex contributor to silencing. It causes all three types. Moreover, as we have also seen, it does so in ways that reinforce the marginalization of those already marginalized.

Let's now consider a third complex contributor: mistakes about other people's emotional states.

§ 7.3 Misinterpreting Emotions

As we have seen many times over, communication is highly inferential. In particular, when figuring out what someone means by what they say, we rely on shared background information. And one of the things that we rely on is the emotional state of the speaker.[21] Let's see this in action.

Reunion Invitee: Lenny and Harim are chatting about an upcoming informal high school reunion when Lenny says, "Nina will be there, you know". Sensing Lenny's anxiety and irritation, Harim realizes that Lenny is complaining about the fact that Nina has been included.

Standing in Line: John is behind Sarah in line for the bar at their grade school reunion, when their mutual friend Peter joins Sarah in conversation. John then taps Peter on the shoulder and says, "Hey dude – no cutting the line!" Recognizing John's cheerfulness and warmth, Peter realizes that John is joking; he is playfully drawing attention to how they all behaved as schoolchildren; Peter recognizes that John's primary intention is to greet his old friend.

In each of these cases, the addressee's correct identification of the speaker's emotional state is crucial in their figuring out the speaker's intended meaning. In *Reunion Invitee*, for example, it is primarily because Harim recognizes that Lenny is upset that Harim realizes that Lenny is here complaining. If Harim had taken Lenny to be joyous on this occasion, he would not have correctly identified Lenny's intended speech action. So, too, in *Standing in Line*. Had John interpreted Peter as angry, he would certainly have understood Peter's utterance differently. It is only because he recognized Peter's warmth toward him that he properly understood Peter's playful speech action.

Clearly, our assessments of others' emotional states inform our communicative inferences. This much is clear. And, for the most part, we are quite good at recognizing facial expressions of emotion, and we are good at doing it even across cultural differences.[22] That said, we do sometimes get it wrong. And, we are more likely to make these sorts of mistakes when we are interacting across social difference.[23]

Why might this be? Well, there are a few explanations for this on offer in the literature. The first concerns cognitive effort. Although we are well *able* to interpret others' facial expressions of emotion, we might not always spend the time and effort to do so to the best of our ability. In other words, we take shortcuts, and one is more likely to spend less effort when one has less to lose as a result of making a mistake. To spell out our first potential explanation: those with more social power tend to have less to lose and so tend to make less of an effort and are thus more likely to get it wrong.[24]

Another possible explanation concerns false stereotypes about the speaker's social group.[25] If a person is influenced by such stereotypes, this can affect how they interpret that speaker's expression of emotion.[26] Empirical studies confirm that cultural beliefs that women are more likely to be sad than angry, for instance, skew the interpretation of women's emotional expression.[27]

A third explanation concerns cultural differences in emotional expression. There are "community-specific style[s] of emotional expression"[28]; some theorists go so far as to posit dialects of expression.[29] If a person is unaware of these community-based differences, they might well misread a speaker's emotional state.

It stands to reason that all of these factors can work together to contribute to mistakes being made. It also stands to reason that sometimes a mistake is just that— a mistake, and it is not caused or explained by anything so systematic.

Let's now consider an example and explore whether and how mistakes about a speaker's emotional state might be a complex contributor to silencing. Here is the example.

Presumed Humility: Stan is the manager at a clothing store where Syndy is a sales person. Stan, who is white, has a tendency to assign Syndy, who is Asian, more than her share of unrewarding work tasks. These tasks are both boring to perform and they keep Syndy off the sales floor thereby preventing her from making sales and thus commissions. One day, Stan realizes that the office supply closet needs to be reorganized, so he suggests that Syndy does it. Fed up with these tasks, Syndy forces a small smile, takes a deep breath, looks Stan in the eye, hands shaking, and says with halting precision, "Stan, while I appreciate your faith in me, it is not my turn; just yesterday, I cleaned all the shelving units in the storage area." Sensing her reluctance, Stan misinterprets it as humility, and he responds reassuringly, "Don't' worry—I know you will do a good job".

In *Presumed Humility* Stan misreads Syndy's emotional state. Although he realizes that she is reluctant to take on the assigned task, he misinterprets the emotion behind that reluctance. Syndy is (justifiably and visibly) angry but Stan interprets her as afraid to mess up the assigned task. That is why, in response, he assures her of his confidence in her ability.

How might Syndy be silenced in this case? Well, for starters, there are recognition failures. Syndy's primary aim in speaking is to object to being assigned another menial task. Although Stan senses her reluctance, he misinterprets her reasons for it. He takes her to be afraid when she is actually angry. Syndy's objecting to the unfairness of her work situation does not register at all with Stan. Stan misidentifies her reasons for objecting and what she is objecting to. As we have seen, each of these types of recognition failures can constitute silencing.

By failing to recognize Syndy's speech action for what it is, Syndy's communicative act is also prevented from having the impact that it ought to have. Rather than assigning this task to someone else and becoming mindful of these fairness issues going forward, as he should do, Stan instead insists that Syndy perform the task. As one can see, Stan's interpretive mistakes prevent Syndy's speech action from realizing its intended worldly impact.

And, finally, Stan's mistake can lead Syndy to self-silence. Precisely because she has here been misunderstood and her efforts seem pointless, she might well be reluctant to try this again. She might also be concerned that Stan's mistakes reinforce false negative stereotypes about women or about Asians. In short, Syndy's decision to self-silence could well be motivated to avoid the resulting harms of doing so.

As one can see, mistakes about a speaker's emotional state can lead to each of the three broad types of silencing. Emotional misinterpretation is thus a complex contributor to silencing. As we can also see, each of the three potential explanations for why we make such mistakes could apply here. Stan might be making less effort to get it right because, as the boss and even as a man, the stakes *for him* are rather low. Stan might also be working with false stereotypes about women or about Asian people. He might be disinclined to recognize anger in women or he might be under the influence of stereotypes about Asian women being submissive. In these ways, false stereotypes about Syndy's group memberships could certainly be contributing to Stan's errors. It could also be that Syndy's way of expressing her emotions is different somewhat from Stan's and Stan fails to realize this. One relevant factor is politeness. As we saw in Chapter 6, less powerful persons are subject to stricter politeness expectations.[30] As an employee, as a women, and as a person of color, this is certainly true of Syndy. If Stan fails to realize how these politeness expectations affect how Syndy expresses her emotions, Stan might mistakenly take her smile as proof positive that she is not angry. After all, Stan never smiles when he is angry (but this is because, as a relatively privileged person, Stan is not socially expected to smile when angry). Blissfully unaware of this, Stan's ignorance of this difference in emotional expression might well interfere with his interpretation of Syndy's emotional state and thus with her speech action.

§ 7.3.1 Anger and Attribution

There is another sort of mistake one can make regarding a speaker's emotion: we can correctly identify the emotion but falsely take it to be unjustified. This happens all too often with women's anger. This kind of mistake can lead to different forms of communicative failure. I shall here identify two.

First, an assertion can be mistaken for a mere expressive speech act. Since expressive speech acts are not known to all, let's first get clear on what those are. Consider the following.

> *Expletives*: Kiel just dropped the elaborate birthday cake he spent two days making. In frustration, he yells a series of inappropriate words. Kiel keeps swearing for a full five minutes.

Swearing is an expressive speech act; what one does when one swears is to manifest how one feels. In this case, Kiel is expressing his supreme frustration. Although swears are a conventional way to express frustration, swearing does not assert anything. What Kiel says does not have truth value. Kiel is not making a claim about the world. Rather, his language use is purely emotive; it enables him to make it clear to others how he is feeling.

Quill Kukla, building on work by Naomi Scheman, argues that women's assertions are sometimes taken up as mere expressives.[31] Let's explore an example of the sort of thing they have in mind.

> *Just Venting*: A harried mother loses it in front of her bewildered husband and children. She kicks the malfunctioning vacuum cleaner and yells "I am sick to death of your mess! As if I have no goals or inner life of my own; everybody else's needs come before mine. One of these days, I am going on strike; I swear to Almighty God and all things sacred, I am that close to flying off to a warm beach and never coming back!"

Here, in *Just Venting*, the family members correctly identify the mother's frustration and anger; it's just that they fail to see it as at all justified. For them, Mommy is just venting; she is like a child having a tantrum; they know from experience that every now and again, she loses it and needs to let off steam. And, when she gets like this, they give her some space. In *Just Venting*, the mom is not interpreted as actually asserting the things she says. Instead, she is interpreted as merely expressing her emotions. Her speech acts of assertion are mistaken as mere expressives. Again, the error here is not the misidentification of her emotional state (they get that right); it's the false belief that her emotions are utterly unwarranted.

Mark Schroeder identifies a similar phenomenon. It concerns mistaken beliefs about what motivates—or causes—a speaker's speech action. Sometimes, this sort of mistake can prevent a speaker's speech action from even being attributed to them. To see the sort of thing he has in mind, let's look at an example.

> *Hangry*: Sarah is furious with her boyfriend, Tom, for spending so much time golfing, instead of helping her with setting up and repairing the antique house they just purchased. She decides to call him on his cell while he is on the back nine. She says, "Tom, we both bought the house so we are both responsible for it. Get your bony ass back here or I'll break every one of those damn golf clubs".

In *Hangry*, Tom knows that Sarah is angry; he also realizes that her anger is warranted. It's just that he thinks that she is suffering from low blood sugar right now and that that is the real reason why she spoke to him as she did. As far as Tom is concerned, it's the low blood sugar speaking here, and not really Sarah. Schroeder calls this 'attributive silencing'. A speaker is attributive silenced when their speech action is not attributed to their own agency. I mentioned it briefly in Chapter 4.[32]

§ 7.4 Conclusion

In this chapter, I have identified three phenomena that are complex contributors to silencing; they each bring about each of the three broad types of silencing. Now, in identifying these three phenomena, I am by no means suggesting that they are the only, or even the most important, complex contributors. There are plenty of others.[33]

8

Communicative Humility

I'll keep this short and sweet. As anyone can see, silencing happens and it happens a lot. In fact, it's all around us. We often misunderstand one another; we routinely make mistakes about whom to believe; and, all too often, we keep silent even when we should speak up. What should be done in light of the ubiquity of silencing?

For starters, it is important to remind ourselves that not all silencing is bad. If an unhelpful snarky comment is misunderstood as a compliment, we have recognition failure silencing. But, in this case anyway, the communicative failure makes our world a slightly better place!

Although silencing *can* have positive effects, it can also be harmful. It can reinforce unjust social hierarchy; it can disempower the already marginalized, and it can undermine our collective quest for knowledge and mutual understanding.

I, for one, would prefer that my actions *do not* contribute to these more harmful forms of silencing. As an individual, though, I certainly do not have the power to stop all harmful forms of silencing. I cannot control the actions of others who misinterpret, discredit, or suppress the speech actions of others. I cannot single-handedly change the social networks that contribute to these harmful forms of silencing, and I cannot undo the stereotypes and biases that play a role either. None of us are individually able to do these things. So, what *can* we do, as individuals?

We can strive to practice what I call 'communicative humility'. In a nutshell, communicative humility involves a commitment to conduct oneself in ways so as to minimize the chances of contributing

On Silencing. Mary Kate McGowan, Oxford University Press. © Mary Kate McGowan 2026.
DOI: 10.1093/9780197837320.003.0008

to harmful instances of silencing. What might this look like in action?

For starters, it will involve being more deliberate in one's communicative exchanges. This includes both speakers and hearers. As we have already seen, speakers should give their interlocutors sufficient clues with respect to intended meaning. When communicating across various kinds of difference, it's risky—even unwarranted—to assume adequate shared understanding. In cases like this, speakers can be more explicit or offer other sorts of clues so as to guide interpretation. In *Yard Sign*, for example, Rose could certainly have done a better job in communicating her meaning to Bill. She could have offered additional clues by saying something like "Signs don't do much, Bill" or "I prefer impactful action". Hearers too should take additional care to get it right under these circumstances. Had Bill stayed aware of the possibility of getting it wrong, he might have asked a clarificatory question before he condemned his neighbor based on his overconfidence in his (mis) interpretation.

Communicative humility also concerns impact prevention. Exercising this kind of humility includes slowing down when assessing the credibility of what one is being told—especially when communicating across various kinds of difference. It involves asking oneself what sort of shortcuts one might be taking and whether those shortcuts are appropriate in context. Jurors, in *Dismissed Witness*, for example, should at least ask themselves whether the social stigma of being unhoused caused them to devalue Claire's testimony. Being aware of credibility deficits and how social bias contributes to them can make us just a little bit more open to the possibility that we are affected too and that we ought to take steps to try to correct for it.

Communication prevention can also sometimes be abated by communicative humility. Being aware of one's social position and how it affects others is a form of humility. And, operating on the assumption that everyone speaks their mind as comfortably as you do is a form of arrogance. Using one's social power to actively make space for those with less social power is one way to exercise communicative humility and quell communication prevention silencing. Signaling to potential (harm avoidance) self-silencers that their speech actions will be properly received is another. To see this, consider again the workplace in *Mad Men*. In that environment, Nora and her co-workers might well decide against trying to report any further instances of sexual harassment but if a male co-worker somehow signals to them that he shares their awareness of the problem, they might well talk to him.[1] These are two ways our humility can prevent harm-avoidance self-silencing and thus avert potentially harmful communicative exchanges.

In short, silencing is everywhere. When it's harmful and when we can do something to make it less so, we should.

Notes

Chapter 1

1. For the claim that pornography subordinates women, see MacKinnon (1987a, 1993). For a speech act analysis of MacKinnon's claim, see Langton (1993). Here are some claims about silencing conservatives on university campuses: "Young liberals believe that they are on the morally righteous side in a culture war and, in order to win, they must silence any form of dissent" (Williams 2019). "For all of their talk of tolerance and social justice and diversity, the political left is, at bottom, all about force. The force to silence dissent" (Kass 2017).
2. These examples come from Maitra and McGowan (2025, chapter 3).
3. This case is inspired by Dotson (2011) drawing from Crenshaw (1991).
4. This example draws from Kukla (2014).
5. For an exploration of being given less credibility than is warranted, see Fricker (2007).
6. The three broad kinds identified here roughly follow, and elaborate on, the three kinds first identified in Langton (1993).

Chapter 2

1. For details, see Grice (1989: 86–116).
2. There are at least two issues with the term 'hearer'. First, it over-generalizes. After all, not all linguistic communication involves the use of sound. We can read text, feel Braille, and see ASL movements. Second, and more worrying, is that by treating spoken language as central or primary, it risks marginalizing people who are hearing impaired. I continue to use the term 'hearer' despite these worries and that's because it's the term used in the literature and there is not yet a suitable replacement.
3. This term is due to Grice (1989).
4. Again, Grice is central here. See Grice (1989: 22–40).
5. Please see note 4.
6. For those unaware, set dancing is a kind of traditional Irish dance.
7. Austin (1975, 1979).
8. Hearers will also come to believe that Dmitri spoke, spoke certain words, committed to the truth of there being a fire on Cypress Street and so on.
9. Intentionalists include Grice (1989) and Strawson (1964); Conventionalists include Austin (1975) and Searle (1969). Some (Harris and McKinney 2021) identify normative theories as a third option, but I see them as a form of Conventionalism. Unnsteinsson (2019) argues for a combo-position and Sbisa (2007) argues persuasively that Austin's Conventionalism concerns the nature of illocution (and not a pre-condition of it).
10. Scanlon (1990: 201).

11. See, for example, Kolodny and Wallace (2003).
12. I thank Quill Kukla for a helpful discussion about this; I found this way of thinking about the main difference between these positions very compelling and I first learned it from them.
13. I thank Rae Langton for helpful discussions of this point. She too emphasizes that one should not assume—as many theorists seem to do—that all speech acts work the same and should thus receive the same theoretical treatment with respect to Intentionalism and Conventionalism.
14. This point about consent is a slightly altered version of a point made by Rae Langton in conversation.

Chapter 3

1. Putnam (1973).
2. This is also the strategy followed in Maitra and McGowan (2025, chapter 3) which this chapter follows closely.
3. See Chapter 1, What Is Silencing?
4. This sort of case is explored in Crenshaw (1991); Dotson (2011).
5. This example is adapted from Kukla (2014: 445).
6. The way I am using the term 'speech', it can include written, spoken, and signed uses of language.
7. Self-expression is another valuable purpose distinct from but overlapping with communication.
8. For a classic statement of this sort of position, see Meiklejohn (1960).
9. This example is adapted from West (2003).
10. Another option is to combine the two conditions and say silencing requires communicative failure resulting from interference. This requirement would still be subject to the concern that interference is insufficiently defined.
11. Again, adapted from West (2003, 2012).
12. As we will see more explicitly in Chapter 5, this notion of impact is unavoidably normative; we are concerned with the impact that a communication ought to have. For details, see § 5.6.
13. A few theorists have offered characterizations of systematicity (McGowan et al. 2016; Maitra 2004; Caponetto 2021).
14. A similar case can be made against including wrongfulness as a necessary condition. In *No Harm, No Foul,* Jonah is not worse off so he is not harmed per se, but he might nevertheless be wronged in virtue of having his self-expression incapacitated or his communicative abilities undermined.
15. Again, more on impact in § 5.6.
16. Again, this broad framework follows Langton (1993).
17. Langton calls this simple silencing but as we shall see in Chapter 6, it is not simple at all (Langton 1993).
18. In a nod to Austin's terminology, Langton calls this 'perlocutionary frustration' (Langton 1993).
19. Some call this illocutionary disablement (Langton 1993; Hornsby 1993). Our focus will be on communication, as opposed to illocution.
20. For details, see § 5.6.
21. Theorists argue that the intentional structure of communication is even more complex than this (Strawson 1964; Schiffer 1988) but this amount of complexity will suffice for our discussion here.

22. I suggest that speaker sincerity is sometimes part of the communicated content (McGowan 2014). Caponetto denies this (Caponetto 2016).

23. See Chapter 2 (§ 2.7) for a discussion of these complexities.

24. Speakers can speaker mean all sorts of things. Consider, for example, Camp's account of insinuation. According to Camp, when a speaker insinuates something, that speaker means what they say explicitly as well as what they insinuate. In addition to this, however, the speaker intends to communicate the off-record nature of the insinuated content as well as the speaker's disposition to deny that content should it be challenged (Camp 2018).

Chapter 4

1. Figuring out what a speaker means is a highly complex process, and there are many ways for it to go awry (Grice 1989). Once we realize this, it's actually pretty surprising that we get things right as often as we do. Some argue that we have evolved to do this well (Sperber and Wilson 2001).

2. Hornsby (1993).

3. Stalnaker (2002).

4. See Friedersdorf (2020) and Schow (2020) for an accessible discussion of a study conducted at the University of North Carolina-Chapel Hill. See Larson et al. (2020) for the report on that study.

5. Internet pile-ons, trolling, and the dissemination of misinformation each contribute to political polarization, the vilification of political opponents, and democratic backsliding. For one explanation of how this works, see Saul (2024). For a discussion of political bias in online censoring, see Barrett (2024).

6. Strictly speaking, these sorts of errors do not themselves constitute communicative failure unless the speaker speaker-means these things. That said, these recognition failures will—in all likelihood—cause the hearer to misidentify the speaker's intended meaning.

7. Steffi Lewis, who told me about this, was quick to point out that the misinterpretation is itself a Joycean stream.

8. Konnikova (2014).

9. This kind of recognition failure came to dominate the original analytic literature on silencing likely in response to an early objection by Jacobson. This focus on this kind of recognition failure led to a narrowing of how Langton and Hornsby's account of silencing was understood. They were concerned with all recognition failures that prevented successful illocution (Langton 1993; Hornsby 1993; Bird 2002; Jacobson 1995).

10. For an exploration what Johnson calls 'confusion mansplaining', see Johnson (2020).

11. Johnson (2020).

12. Solnit (2014); the term 'mansplaining's is attributed to Solnit but it seems she did not coin it. I am also reluctant to say that she is the first to write about it. My hunch is that many have but just didn't get credit for it.

13. These recognition failures interact in complex ways; they can also cause one another.

14. Hornsby (1993); McGowan (2014); Caponetto (2016).

15. I am open to the possibility that with promises, speaker sincerity is always—at least to some extent—speaker-meant.

16. For an accessible exploration of male entitlement, see Manne (2020).
17. McGowan (2014) calls it 'sincerity silencing'.
18. This will be discussed below. See also note 9.
19. *DPP v. Morgan* (1976).
20. Morgan denied telling them this; it was part of the defense for the three men who were tried for rape.
21. *DPP v. Morgan* (1976). In this case, the jury did not believe that the three men failed to recognize the sincerity of Mrs. Morgan's refusals but—troublingly—the court instructed that a false and even unreasonable belief in consent is sufficient to preclude a rape conviction.
22. This is but a sampling: MacKinnon (1987a, 1993); Langton (1993, 2009); Hornsby (1993); Green (1998); West (2003); McGowan (2003, 2019); Saul (2006); Scoccia (1996); Eaton (2007); Maitra (2009, 2012); Maitra and McGowan (2010); McKinney (2016); McGowan et al. (2016); Mikkola (2011); Langton (1998); Spewak (2023); Unnsteinsson (2019); Emerick (2019); Jacobson (1995); Bird (2002); McGowan (2014, 2009, 2017); West (2012); Langton and West (1999); Caponetto (2016, 2021, 2017); Wieland (2007); Wyatt (2009); Finlayson (2014); Bauer (2015); Sbisa (n.d.).
23. MacKinnon (1993, 2012).
24. Rowles (2015).
25. They also fail to recognize her intended speech action; they fail to recognize that she intends to terminate the meeting. If a speaker is taken to be joking when they are not, their serious speech action is mistaken for a non-serious one. This notion of seriousness is discussed more in § 4.5.
26. Although other philosophical traditions have long engaged with issues concerning language and social power, this book works within the analytic philosophical tradition, which has recently had an upsurge on this topic. For explicit discussion of "authority silencing" in analytic feminism, see McGowan (2009); Caponetto (2017) and Mason (2023).
27. Here, Peter seems to attribute Harriet's complaints to the PMS and thus not to Harriet. He treats Harriet as if she is under the influence of PMS and thus not really responsible for what she is saying. Mark Schroeder calls this 'attributive silencing' (Schroeder 2022).
28. Schroeder (2022).
29. Caponetto (2016, 2021).
30. Bach and Harnish (1979).
31. The non-seriousness of some contexts are signaled by convention (e.g., being on a stage in a darkened theater); otherwise, speakers have a responsibility to signal it to their audience (e.g., through intonation or a raised brow).
32. Davidson (1979); Langton (1993); Caponetto (2016, 2021).
33. Langton (1993: 316).
34. Caponetto (2016, 2021).
35. Of course, Langton is also correct that *Fire Warning* is an instance of illocutionary uptake failure; Langton never claimed that all of the cases she identifies work in the exact same way (Langton 1993).
36. Caponetto (2016: 188, 2021: 196).
37. Horisk (2024: 161) leaves open the possibility that joke-tellings are some kind of illocution. Alward (2009) considers three hypotheses regarding the illocutions of stage actors.
38. This might well be all Caponetto means when she says that such speakers are not illocuting at all.
39. When watching a theatrical performance, we are encouraged to suspend our awareness of the above indirection. That is, we are invited to think of ourselves

as observers of a real-life scene, one that, at some level, we know is merely being play acted before us and for our benefit. The same could plausibly be said for jurors during a trial; jurors are not always aware of being the primarily intended audience; thinking of themselves instead as passive observers of the unfolding courtroom drama.

40. Levinson (1979).

41. Clark and Carlson (1982). See also Lewiński (2021).

42. As evidence that these informatives are operative, Clark and Carlson point out Nora's recognition of that promise is subsequently relied on by everyone in that conversation. After all, this is how updating works.

43. One might require that (proper) illocution requires that a speaker be performing illocutionary acts in addition to, and distinct from, any informatives being performed. I thank Laura Caponetto for stressing this possibility.

44. These background assumptions are sometimes called 'pragmatic presuppositions' (Stalnaker 1974).

45. Lewis (1978). We can learn a lot about the world and ourselves through fiction. Austen's *Pride and Prejudice*, for instance, teaches us a lot about Victorian England and Morrison's *Beloved* teaches us about the depth of devastation of chattel slavery. Some (Mahon 2019) deny that fictions can make assertions.

46. We might wonder who the real speaker is. Although Latisha is the person uttering the words (that presuppose these things), those words were actually written by someone else. And, while Latisha adds her own finesse to her performance of the utterance-tokens, that finesse is guided and even constrained by directors, producers, and others. Similar questions arise concerning speech acts performed in pornography. Who is the speaker? If pornography is fiction, can it assert falsehoods about women? Can it enact harmful social norms, as some contend? (MacKinnon 1993; Langton 1993; Langton and West 1999).

47. Some argue that pornography causes some consumers to make this very sort of mistake. Consider Maitra (2009); Wieland (2007); Wyatt (2009); Hesni (2018).

48. There is another important difference between an actor on a stage and a person (taken to be) following a social script. With the social script situation, the person doing the interpreting (in this case, Lou) takes himself to be a participant in that very social script. He misinterprets Tina as making a move in that script and Lou plans to make the next move. When watching a play, by contrast, we are mere observers; we are not interacting with the actor; we are not ourselves an actor in the play.

49. McGowan (2009); Mason (2023).

Chapter 5

1. This example is based on Akinlade (2020).

2. Meghani et al. (2012).

3. Mather, after corroborating what Onesimus told him with other enslaved persons, convinced a prominent Boston doctor, Zabdiel Boylston, to inoculate. Of the 287 people inoculated by Dr. Boylston, only 2% died of small pox, compared to an almost 15% mortality for the general population (Niederhuber 2014; Boylston 2012; Smith 2021).

4. These credibility judgments will be discussed in more detail in § 5.6.

5. Telling is an information-sharing speech act. Not all factual statements are instances of telling. Pleasantries exchanged out of politeness (e.g., "it's a beautiful day" said to

a fellow walker) are not acts of telling since they do not seek to impart desired information to the addressee. For details, see Lackey (2008).

6. There are alternative accounts of what we are committing to when we assert things but the details do not matter for current purposes. See Stalnaker (2002) for one such alternative account.

7. Medina (2011); Davis (2016).

8. Collins (2000).

9. Dotson (2011).

10. Longino (1990).

11. Fricker (2007).

12. Fricker (2007); when these deficits are systematic, it can be a form of epistemic violence (Dotson 2011). It might also be a what some (Darwall 1977; Waldron 2012) call a dignitary harm.

13. This phenomenon is called 'intersectionality'. For a classic on this, see Crenshaw (1989).

14. Sometimes, we make sounds that do not have any conventional meaning and when we do so, our utterance fails to have locutionary force.

15. Langton (1993).

16. Apologies are interesting and rich speech acts. For a helpful discussion about that richness, see Bovens (2008).

17. Readers might well disagree with me about particular cases.

18. As we will see more explicitly in Chapter 5, this notion of impact is unavoidably normative; we are concerned with the impact that a communication ought to have. For details, see § 5.5.

19. David Spewak distinguishes linguistic causal effects from extra-linguistic ones and argues that being illegitimately prevented from affecting the conversation in which one is participating constitutes a form of perlocutionary silencing (Spewak 2023).

20. MacKinnon (1987a, 1993); MacKinnon and Dworkin (1997).

21. Parent (1990).

22. It's not the only way. For others, see Vadas and Journal of Philosophy Inc. (1987); McGowan (2003).

23. Langton (1993); Hornsby (1993). Although they offer a similar account of silencing, Hornsby and Langton explore different potential connections between pornography consumption and silencing. For Hornsby, it's a causal connection. Langton explores the possibility of a constitutive connection, of pornography enacting the norms governing speech acts. For details, see Langton (1993).

24. Plenty of other recognition failures are also possible and possibly caused by pornography consumption. For empirical work on the harms of pornography consumption, see Waltman (2021).

25. Finlayson (2014).

26. Jacobson (1995); Bird (2002); Wieland (2007); Finlayson (2014).

27. There are complexities and controversies in the background here. For details, see Anderson (2005a, 2005b); MacKinnon (2016); Caponetto (2017); Kukla (2018).

28. See Mason (2023) for an exploration of different kinds of authority and their context-sensitive fragility.

29. Refusal is distinct from resistance. A refusal is an authoritative and essentially normative communicative act; it denies permission. Resistance is different; it is usually physical—to resist is to fight back or run away. A sexual refusal ought to be sufficient to prevent rape. When there is impact silencing, it is not sufficient. Unfortunately, the resistance is all too often undermined by fear, shock, and physical differences.

30. Some go so far as to argue that the perpetrators' awareness of the victim's lack of consent is required for the *mens rea* of rape (and that recognition failure silencing actually undermines the moral and legal responsibility of rapists) (Wieland 2007).

31. As MacKinnon would have it, pornography consumption plays an important role in the sexual abuse of women. For additional empirical support, see Waltman (2021).
32. It is not just women who have their sexual refusals impact silenced but it is mostly women. See Waltman (2021).
33. Hearth (2014: ix).

Chapter 6

1. Langton called this 'simple silencing', although, as we shall soon see, it is far from simple (Langton 1993).
2. This notion of prevention is causal-explanatory; it concerns what causes a certain communication to not happen. As such, it involves unavoidable subjectivity and relativity. This is because we are interested in the *explanatorily relevant* cause; in other words, we are interested in what we do not know but want to know about the complex objective causal web leading to what does in fact happen (and thus also to what does not happen). These issues are related to my concerns about relying too heavily on an underspecified notion of interference.
3. Please see previous note.
4. Although I build harm (the anticipation of which motivates the speaker's decision against speaking) into the characterization of harm-avoidance self-silencing, I here remain agnostic about whether it itself is harmful.
5. Similar issues are explored in McGowan (2018).
6. I thank Sally Thach for recommending that I consider this sort of example.
7. It's possible that with further details specified, the disagreement Tom anticipates in *Unionization* is harmful.
8. In treating being socially shunned as a potential harm, I am by no means suggesting that others owe us friendship. Not being friends with someone is not the same as pro-actively harassing and shunning them. I thank Quill Kukla for encouraging me to make this point explicit.
9. Dotson (2011).
10. Arguably, the reasonable person standard in law tends to favor a privileged white man perspective. For a discussion of how such considerations affect the fighting words principle, see Greenawalt (1996).
11. Dotson (2011).
12. This case is inspired by Dotson (2011) drawing from Crenshaw (1991).
13. For linguistic work on AAE, see Lippi-Green (1997); Rickford (2015); and Green (2002). For an exploration of silencing and AAE, see Foster (2020) and Rickford and King (2016). AAE is discussed in more detail in § 7.1.
14. This case is similar to one in Mason (2023), where Mason argues that these heightened politeness expectations mean that women actually lack the authority to refuse.
15. For a fictional account of this, Roupenian (2017), and for real cases, Bennett and Jones (2018). For more theoretical explorations, see Cahill (2016); Dougherty (2022); and Mason (2023).
16. One can certainly make a case that politeness norms in general cause self-silencing on the grounds that a desire to avoid counting as rude interferes with people's communicative capacities. In § 6.1.3, we understood self-silencing as involving harm avoidance and counting as rude is not always harmful. When elevated and unjust politeness norms are operative, however, counting as rude can be harmful.

Chapter 7

1. In this discussion, I am not distinguishing between causing silencing and constituting it. This distinction matters a lot in some contexts. For a discussion of why it matters and how to draw the distinction, see Langton (1993) developing MacKinnon (1987b, 1993). See also McGowan (2019) and Caponetto and Cepollaro (2021).
2. Accent concerns only pronunciation, intonation, and the rhythm of speaking; dialect concerns additional features (like vocabulary, grammar, and syntax). For an accessible introduction, see Boyanton (2024).
3. Green (2002: 5-8); Lanehart (2022: 41-57).
4. Pullum (1999).
5. Lippi-Green (1997: 110). I focus on dialectical differences in the United States but this is part of a more general pattern. Consider, for example, how regional or "foreign" accents can affect a speaker's perceived credibility.
6. For an exploration of the silencing of AAE speakers, see Foster (2020). For a discussion of AAE and perjury law, see (Maitra and McGowan 2025) ch 12 available online at https://global.oup.com/us/companionwebsites/9780190929022/.
7. For a similar real word case, see Jones et al. (2019: e221). For analysis of AAE testimony in an actual trial, see Rickford and King (2016).
8. Regarding the richness of verb tenses in AAE versus SAE, Toni Morrison said "It's terrible to think that a child with five different present tenses comes to school to be faced with books that are less than his own language. And then to be told things about his language, which is him, that are sometimes permanently damaging. He may never know the etymology of Africanisms in his language, not even that 'hip' is a real word or that 'the dozens' mean something. This is a really cruel fall-out of racism. I know the standard English. I want to use it to help restore the other language, the lingua franca". Cited in J. Rickford and Rickford (2000).
9. No doubt racism is playing a role here, contributing to the ease with which such negative conclusions are drawn. I thank Taylor Quaye for suggesting that this be made explicit.
10. § 4.1.4.
11. For an exploration of AAE in the court system, see Rickford and King (2016) and Foster (2020).
12. Pohlhaus (2012); Berenstain (2020).
13. Many refer to this as 'hermeneutical injustice', an expression coined by Fricker (2007). Conceptual impoverishment also includes conceptual distortion (Jenkins 2017; Mason 2021).
14. Spender (1980); Hornsby (1995); Fricker (2007).
15. Spender (1980: 54-58).
16. I am here concerned with difficulties communicating *to the non-marginalized* (or even the less marginalized). Those with similar experiences can rely on that shared experience to successfully communicate. See Medina (2013).
17. The landmark case here is *Meritor Savings Bank v. Vinson* (1986).
18. We are here concerned with the legal notion of hostile environment workplace harassment; the socially shared concept of gender-based workplace harassment has a longer history and one that differs across sub-communities. For an intersectional exploration, see Berenstain (2020).
19. Before it was a socially shared concept, women who experienced such harassment had difficulty recognizing it as such (Fricker 2007: 153). In other cases, marginalized persons communicate perfectly well with one another but face challenges in communicating their experiences with members of a privileged group

(Medina 2013; Fricker 2016). For an exploration of how other epistemic resources are shaped by social position, see Pohlhaus (2012) and Dotson (2012).

20. Yes, this is a nod to the popular AMC television program Mad Men.
21. Trip (Glazer 2019) argues for what he calls 'emotional misperception', a kind of epistemic injustice that can constitute non-linguistic communicative interference. In this book, I am focusing on linguistic communication so my concern is with how these mistakes about a speaker's emotional state can contribute to (linguistic) communicative interference and thus silencing. For a discussion of the difference between linguistic and non-linguistic communication, see Chapter 2 (§ 2.1).
22. Elfenbein and Ambady (2002).
23. Elfenbein and Ambady (2002).
24. Glazer (2019); Henley (1986).
25. For a discussion of stereotypes and how they can affect our perceptions and judgments, see Blum (2004).
26. Glazer (2019).
27. Plant et al. (2000) are careful to study both beliefs about gendered differences in the experience of emotions as well as their expression.
28. Glazer (2019: 61).
29. Elfenbein and Ambady (2002); Elfenbein et al. (2007).
30. Specifically, see § 6.5.
31. Kukla (2014); Scheman (1980).
32. § 4.4.3.
33. Consider, for instance, the discussion of seriousness silencing in § 4.5.

Chapter 8

1. As Kristie Dotson has emphasized, hearers should signal competence in order to preclude harmful instances of testimonial smothering (a form of harm-avoidance self-silencing) (Dotson 2011).

References

Akinlade, Oluwafunmilayo. 2020. "Taking Black Pain Seriously." *New England Journal of Medicine* 383 (10). https://www.nejm.org/doi/10.1056/NEJMpv 2024759.

Alward, Peter. 2009. "Onstage Illocution." *The Journal of Aesthetics and Art Critcism* 67 (3): 321–31.

Anderson, Michelle. 2005a. "All-American Rape." *St. John's Law Review* 79 (3): 625–44.

Anderson, Michelle. 2005b. "Negotiating Sex." *Southern California Law Review* 78 (6): 101–40.

Austin, J.L. 1975. *How to Do Things with Words*. 2nd ed, edited by J.O. Urmson and Marina Sbisà. The William James Lectures. Harvard University Press.

Austin, J.L. 1979. "Performative Utterances." In *Philosophical Papers*, edited by J.O. Urmson and G.J. Warnock. Clarendon Press.

Bach, Kent, and Robert M. Harnish. 1979. *Linguistic Communication and Speech Acts*. MIT Press.

Barrett, Paul. 2024. "More Evidence That Conservatives Are Not Unfairly Censored on Social Media." *QuickTake:NYU Stern*, October 3. https://bhr.stern.nyu.edu/quick-take/more-evidence-that-conservatives-are-not-unfairly-censored-on-social-media/.

Bauer, Nancy. 2015. *How to Do Things with Pornography*. Harvard University Press.

Bennett, Jessica, and Daniel Jones. 2018. "45 Stories of Sex and Consent on Campus." *New York Times*, May 10. https://www.nytimes.com/interactive/2018/05/10/style/sexual-consent-college-campus.html.

Berenstain, Nora. 2020. "White Feminist Gaslighting." *Hypatia* 35 (4): 733–58. https://doi.org/10.1017/hyp.2020.31.

Bird, Alexander. 2002. "Illocutionary Silencing." *Pacific Philosophical Quarterly* 83 (1): 1–15. https://doi.org/10.1111/1468-0114.00137.

Blum, Lawrence. 2004. "Stereotypes and Stereotyping: A Moral Analysis." *Philosophical Papers* 33 (3): 251–89. https://doi.org/10.1080/0556864040 9485143.

Bovens, Luc. 2008. "Apologies." *Proceedings of the Aristotelian Society (Hardback)* 108 (1pt3): 219–39. https://doi.org/10.1111/j.1467-9264.2008.00244.x.

Boyanton, Megan Ulu-Lani. 2024. "A Brief History of the United States' Accents and Dialects." *Smithsonian*, January 17. https://www.smithsonian mag.com/history/a-brief-history-of-the-united-states-accents-and-diale cts-180983591/.

Boylston, Arthur. 2012. "The Origins of Inoculation." *Journal of the Royal Society of Medicine* 105 (7): 309–13. https://doi.org/10.1258/ jrsm.2012.12k044.

Cahill, Ann J. 2016. "Unjust Sex vs. Rape." *Hypatia* 31 (4): 746–61. https://doi. org/10.1111/hypa.12294.

Camp, Elisabeth. 2018. "Insinuation, Common Ground, and the Conversational Record." In *New Work on Speech Acts*, edited by Daniel Fogal, Daniel W. Harris, and Matt Moss. Oxford University Press.

Caponetto, Laura. 2016. "Silencing Speech with Pornography." *Phenomenology and Mind*, no. 11: 11. https://doi.org/10.13128/Phe_Mi-20118.

Caponetto, Laura. 2017. "On Silencing, Authority, and the Act of Refusal." *Rivista Di Estetica* 64 (1): 64. https://doi.org/10.4000/estetica.2061.

Caponetto, Laura. 2021. "A Comprehensive Definition of Illocutionary Silencing." *Topoi* 40 (1): 191–202. https://doi.org/10.1007/s11 245-020-09705-2.

Caponetto, Laura, and Bianca Cepollaro. 2021. "'Discrimination Preferred': How Ordinary Verbal Bigotry Harms." *Australasian Philosophical Review* 5 (2): 189–95. https://doi.org/10.1080/24740500.2021.2012102.

Clark, Herbert, and Thomas Carlson. 1982. "Hearers and Speech Acts." *Language* 58 (2): 332–74.

Collins, Patricia Hill. 2000. *Black Feminist Thought: Knowledge, Consciousness, and the Politics of Empowerment*. Rev. 10th anniversary ed. Routledge.

Crenshaw, Kimberle. 1989. "Demarginalizing the Intersection of Race and Sex: A Black Feminist Critique of Antidiscrimination Doctrine, Feminist Theory and Antiracist Politics." *University of Chicago Legal Forum* 1 (8): 139–67.

Crenshaw, Kimberle. 1991. "Mapping the Margins: Intersectionality, Identity Politics, and Violence Against Women of Color." *Stanford Law Review* 43 (6): 1241–99.

Darwall, Stephen. 1977. "Two Kinds of Respect." *Ethics* 88 (1): 36–49.

Davidson, Donald. 1979. "Communication and Convention." *Synthese* 59 (1): 3–17.

Davis, Emmalon. 2016. "Typecasts, Tokens, and Spokespersons: A Case for Credibility Excess as Testimonial Injustice." *Hypatia* 31 (3): 485–501.

Dotson, Kristie. 2011. "Tracking Epistemic Violence, Tracking Practices of Silencing." *Hypatia* 26 (2): 236–57. https://doi.org/10.1111/ j.1527-2001.2011.01177.x.

Dotson, Kristie. 2012. "A Cautionary Tale: On Limiting Epistemic Oppression." *Frontiers: A Journal of Women Studies* 33 (1): 24–47. https:// doi.org/10.5250/fronjwomestud.33.1.0024.

Dougherty, Tom. 2022. "Social Constraints on Sexual Consent." *Politics, Philosophy & Economics* 21 (4): 393–414. https://doi.org/10.1177/147059 4X221114620.

DPP v. Morgan (House of Lords, UKHL 3 1976).

Eaton, A. W. 2007. "A Sensible Antiporn Feminism." *Ethics* 117 (4): 674–715. https://doi.org/10.1086/519226.

Elfenbein, Hillary Anger, and Nalini Ambady. 2002. "On the Universality and Cultural Specificity of Emotion Recognition: A Meta-Analysis." *Psychological Bulletin* 128 (2): 203–35. https://doi.org/10.1037/ 0033-2909.128.2.203.

Elfenbein, Hillary Anger, Martin Beaupré, Manon Lévesque, and Ursula Hess. 2007. "Toward a Dialect Theory: Cultural Differences in the Expression and Recognition of Posed Facial Expressions." *Emotion* 7 (1): 131–46. https://doi.org/10.1037/1528-3542.7.1.131.

Emerick, Barrett. 2019. "The Violence of Silencing." In *Pacifism, Politics, and Feminism: Intersections and Innovations*, edited by Jennifer Kling. Brill.

Finlayson, Lorna. 2014. "How to Screw Things with Words." *Hypatia* 29 (4): 774–89. https://doi.org/10.1111/hypa.12109.

Foster, Edilia. 2020. "Not Talking Black: African American Vernacular English and Dialect-Based Smothering." Wellesley College.

Fricker, Miranda. 2007. *Epistemic Injustice: Power and the Ethics of Knowing.* Oxford University Press.

Fricker, Miranda. 2016. "Epistemic Injustice and the Preservation of Ignorance." In *The Epistemic Dimensions of Ignorance*, edited by Rik Peels and Martijn Blaauw. Cambridge University Press. https://doi.org/10.1017/ 9780511820076.

Friedersdorf, Conor. 2020. "Evidence That Conservative Students Really Do Self-Censor: Is Free Speech Imperiled on American College Campuses?" *The Atlantic*, February.

Glazer, Trip. 2019. "Epistemic Violence and Emotional Misperception." *Hypatia* 34 (1): 59–75. https://doi.org/10.1111/hypa.12455.

Green, Leslie. 1998. "Pornographizing, Subordinating, and Silencing." In *Censorship and Silencing: Practices of Cultural Regulation*, edited by Robert C. Post. Getty Research Institute.

Green, Lisa J. 2002. *African American English: A Linguistic Introduction.* Cambridge University Press.

Greenawalt, Kent. 1996. *Fighting Words: Individuals, Communities, and Liberties of Speech.* Princeton University Press.

Grice, Paul. 1989. *Studies in the Way of Words.* Harvard University Press.

Harris, Daniel, and Rachel McKinney. 2021. "Speect-Act Theory: Social and Political Applications." In *The Routledge Handbook of Social and Political Philosophy of Language*, edited by Justin Khoo and Rachel Katharine Sterken. Routledge.

Hearth, Amy Hill. 2014. *"Strong Medicine." Speaks: A Native American Elder Has Her Say.* Atria Books.

Henley, Nancy M. 1986. *Body Politics: Power, Sex, and Nonverbal Communication.* 1st Touchstone ed. A Touchstone Book. Simon & Schuster.

Hesni, Samia. 2018. "Illocutionary Frustration." *Mind* 127 (508): 947–76. https://doi.org/10.1093/mind/fzy033.

Horisk, Claire. 2024. *Dangerous Jokes: How Racism and Sexism Weaponize Humor.* Oxford University Press.

Hornsby, Jennifer. 1993. "Speech Acts and Pornography." *Women's Philosophy Review* 10: 38–45.

Hornsby, Jennifer. 1995. "Disempowered Speech." *Philosophical Topics* 23 (2): 127–47. https://doi.org/10.5840/philtopics199523211.

Jacobson, Daniel. 1995. "Freedom of Speech Acts? A Response to Langton." *Philosophy & Public Affairs* 24 (1): 64–78. https://doi.org/10.1111/j.1088-4963.1995.tb00022.x.

Jenkins, Katharine. 2017. "Rape Myths and Domestic Abuse Myths as Hermeneutical Injustices." *Journal of Applied Philosophy* 34 (2): 191–205. https://doi.org/10.1111/japp.12174.

Johnson, Casey Rebecca. 2020. "Mansplaining and Illocutionary Force." *Feminist Philosophy Quarterly* 6 (4). https://doi.org/10.5206/fpq/2020.4.8168.

Jones, Taylor, Jessica Rose Kalbfeld, Ryan Hancock, and Robin Clark. 2019. "Testifying While Black: An Experimental Study of Court Reporter Accuracy in Transcription of African American English." *Language* 95 (2): e216–52. https://doi.org/10.1353/lan.2019.0042.

Kass, John. 2017. "Leftist Foes Silence Foes at Berkeley, Where Free Speech Movement Was Born." *Chicago Tribune*, February 2. https://www.chicagotribune.com/columns/john-kass/ct-free-speech-berkeley-kass-0203-20170202-column.html.

Kolodny, Niko, and R. Jay Wallace. 2003. "Promises and Practices Revisited." *Philosophy & Public Affairs* 31 (2): 119–54.

Konnikova, Maria. 2014. "Excuse While I Kiss This Guy." *The New Yorker*, December. https://www.newyorker.com/science/maria-konnikova/science-misheard-lyrics-mondegreens.

Kukla, Rebecca. 2014. "Performative Force, Convention, and Discursive Injustice." *Hypatia* 29 (2): 440–57. https://doi.org/10.1111/j.1527-2001.2012.01316.x.

Kukla, Rebecca. 2018. "That's What She Said: The Language of Sexual Negotiation." *Ethics* 129 (1): 70–97. https://doi.org/10.1086/698733.

Lackey, Jennifer. 2008. *Learning from Words: Testimony as a Source of Knowledge.* Oxford University Press.

Lanehart, Sonja. 2022. *Language in African American Communities.* Routledge. https://doi.org/10.4324/9781003204756.

Langton, Rae. 1993. "Speech Acts and Unspeakable Acts." *Philosophy and Public Affairs* 22 (4): 293–330.

Langton, Rae. 1998. "Subordination, Silence, and Pornography's Authority." In *Censorship and Silencing: Practices of Cultural Regulation*, edited by Robert C. Post. Getty Research Institute for the History of Art and the Humanities.

Langton, Rae. 2009. *Sexual Solipsism: Philosophical Essays on Pornography and Objectification*. Oxford University Press.

Langton, Rae, and Caroline West. 1999. "Scorekeeping in a Pornographic Language Game." *Australasian Journal of Philosophy* 77 (3): 303–19. https://doi.org/10.1080/00048409912349061.

Larson, Jennifer, Mark McNeilly, and Timothy J. Ryan. 2020. *Free Expression and Constructive Dialogue at the Unversity of North Caroline at Chapel Hill.* https://fecdsurveyreport.web.unc.edu/wp-content/uploads/sites/22160/2020/02/UNC-Free-Expression-Report.pdf.

Levinson, Stephen C. 1979. "Activity Types and Language." *Linguistics* 17: 365–99.

Lewiński, Marcin. 2021. "Illocutionary Pluralism." *Synthese* 199 (3–4): 6687–714. https://doi.org/10.1007/s11229-021-03087-7.

Lewis, David. 1978. "Truth in Fiction." *American Philosophical Quarterly* 15 (1): 37–46.

Lippi-Green, Rosina. 1997. *English with an Accent: Language, Ideology, and Discrimination in the United States.* Routledge.

Longino, Helen E. 1990. *Science as Social Knowledge: Values and Objectivity in Scientific Inquiry.* Princeton Paperbacks Philosophy of Science. Princeton University Press.

MacKinnon, Catharine A. 1987a. *Feminism Unmodified: Discourses on Life and Law.* Harvard University Press.

MacKinnon, Catharine A. 1987b. "Francis Biddle's Sister: Pornography, Civil Rights, and Speech." In *Feminism Unmodified: Discourses on Life and Law.* Harvard University Press.

MacKinnon, Catharine A. 1993. *Only Words.* Harvard University Press.

MacKinnon, Catharine A. 2012. "Foreword." In *Speech and Harm: Controversies over Free Speech*, edited by Ishani Maitra and Mary Kate McGowan. Oxford University Press.

MacKinnon, Catharine A. 2016. "Rape Redefined." *Harvard Law & Policy Review* 10 (2): 431–77.

MacKinnon, Catharine A., and Andrea Dworkin, eds. 1997. *In Harm's Way: The Pornography Civil Rights Hearings.* Harvard University Press.

Mahon, James. 2019. "Novels Never Lie." *British Journal of Aesthetics* 59 (3): 323–38.

Maitra, Ishani. 2004. "Silence and Responsibility." *Philosophical Perspectives* 18 (1): 189–208. https://doi.org/10.1111/j.1520-8583.2004.00025.x.

Maitra, Ishani. 2009. "Silencing Speech." *Canadian Journal of Philosophy* 39 (2): 309–38. https://doi.org/10.1353/cjp.0.0050.

Maitra, Ishani. 2012. "Subordinating Speech." In *Speech and Harm: Controversies over Free Speech*, edited by Ishani Maitra and Mary Kate McGowan. Oxford University Press.

Maitra, Ishani, and Mary Kate McGowan. 2010. "On Silencing, Rape, and Responsibility." *Australasian Journal of Philosophy* 88 (1): 167–72. https://doi.org/10.1080/00048400902941331.

Maitra, Ishani, and Mary Kate McGowan. 2025. *Words in Action: An Introduction to the Social Philosophy of Language.* Oxford University Press.

Manne, Kate. 2020. *Entitled: How Male Privilege Hurts Women.* Crown.

Mason, Elinor. 2023. "Sexual Refusal: The Fragility of Women's Authority." *Hypatia* 38 (1): 114–33. https://doi.org/10.1017/hyp.2023.7.

Mason, Rebecca. 2021. "Hermeneutical Injustice." In *The Routledge Handbook of Social and Political Philosophy of Language*, edited by Justin Khoo and Rachel Sterken. Routledge Handbooks in Philosophy. Routledge, Taylor & Francis Group.

McGowan, Mary Kate. 2003. "Conversational Exercitives and the Force of Pornography." *Philosophy & Public Affairs* 31 (2): 155–89. https://doi.org/10.1111/j.1088-4963.2003.00155.x.

McGowan, Mary Kate. 2009. "On Silencing and Sexual Refusal." *Journal of Political Philosophy* 17 (4): 487–94. https://onlinelibrary.wiley.com/doi/10.1111/j.1467-9760.2009.00346.x.

McGowan, Mary Kate. 2014. "Sincerity Silencing." *Hypatia* 29 (2): 458–73. https://doi.org/10.1111/hypa.12034.

McGowan, Mary Kate. 2017. "On Multiple Types of Silencing." In *Beyond Speech: Pornography and Analytic Feminist Philosophy*, edited by Mari Mikkola. Oxford University Press.

McGowan, Mary Kate. 2018. "On Political Correctness, Microaggressions, and Silencing in the Academy." In *Academic Freedom*, edited by Jennifer Lackey. Oxford University Press. https://doi.org/10.1093/oso/9780198791508.003.0008.

McGowan, Mary Kate. 2019. *Just Words: On Speech and Hidden Harm.* Oxford University Press.

McGowan, Mary Kate, Ilana Walder-Biesanz, Morvareed Rezaian, and Chloe Emerson. 2016. "On Silencing and Systematicity: The Challenge of the Drowning Case." *Hypatia* 31 (1): 74–90. https://doi.org/10.1111/hypa.12224.

McKinney, Rachel Ann. 2016. "Extracted Speech." *Social Theory and Practice* 42 (2): 258–84. https://doi.org/10.5840/soctheorpract201642215.

Medina, José. 2011. "The Relevance of Credibility Excess in a Proportional View of Epistemic Injustice: Differential Epistemic Authority and the Social

Imaginary." *Social Epistemology* 25 (1): 15–35. https://doi.org/10.1080/ 02691728.2010.534568.

Medina, José. 2013. *The Epistemology of Resistance: Gender and Racial Oppression, Epistemic Injustice, and Resistant Imaginations.* Studies in Feminist Philosophy. Oxford University Press.

Meghani, Salimah H., Eeeseung Byun, and Rollin M. Gallagher. 2012. "Time to Take Stock: A Meta-Analysis and Systematic Review of Analgesic Treatment Disparities for Pain in the United States." *Pain Medicine (Malden, Mass.)* 13 (2): 150–74. https://doi.org/10.1111/j.1526-4637.2011.01310.x.

Meiklejohn, Alexander. 1960. "Free Speech and Its Relation to Self-Government." In *Political Freedom: The Constitutional Powers of the People.* Harper.

Meritor Savings Bank v. Vinson, 477 U.S. 59 (United States Supreme Court 1986).

Mikkola, Mari. 2011. "Illocution, Silencing, and the Act of Refusal." *Pacific Philosophical Quarterly* 92 (3): 415–37. https://onlinelibrary.wiley.com/ doi/10.1111/j.1468-0114.2011.01404.x.

Niederhuber, Matthew. 2014. "The Fight Over Inoculation During the 1721 Boston Smallpoox Elidemic." *Harvard University The Gradute School of Arts and Sciences Blog.* https://sitn.hms.harvard.edu/flash/special-edition-on-infectious-disease/2014/the-fight-over-inoculation-during-the-1721-boston-smallpox-epidemic/.

Parent, W. A. 1990. "A Second Look at Pornography and The Subordination of Women." *The Journal of Philosophy* 87 (4): 205. https://doi.org/10.2307/ 2026681.

Plant, E. Ashby, Janet Shibley Hyde, Dacher Keltner, and Patricia G. Devine. 2000. "The Gender Stereotyping of Emotions." *Psychology of Women Quarterly* 24 (1): 81–92. https://doi.org/10.1111/j.1471-6402.2000.tb01 024.x.

Pohlhaus, Gaile. 2012. "Relational Knowing and Epistemic Injustice: Toward a Theory of *Willful Hermeneutical Ignorance*." *Hypatia* 27 (4): 715–35. https://doi.org/10.1111/j.1527-2001.2011.01222.x.

Pullum, Geoffrey. 1999. "African American Vernacular English Is Not Standard English with Mistakes." In *The Workings of Language: From Prescriptions to Perspectives.*, edited by Rebecca S. Wheeler. Praeger.

Putnam, Hilary. 1973. "Meaning and Reference." *The Journal of Philosophy* 70 (19): 699. https://doi.org/10.2307/2025079.

Rickford, John R. 2015. "African American Vernacular English in California: Over Four Decades of Vibrant Variationist Research." In *The Oxford Handbook of African American Language*, edited by Jennifer Bloomquist, Lisa J. Green, and Sonja L. Lanehart. Oxford University Press. https://doi.org/10.1093/oxfordhb/9780199795390.013.32.

Rickford, John R., and Sharese King. 2016. "Language and Linguistics on Trial: Hearing Rachel Jeantel (and Other Vernacular Speakers) in the Courtroom and Beyond." *Language* 92 (4): 948–88. https://doi.org/10.1353/lan.2016.0078.

Rickford, John, and Russell Rickford. 2000. "In Praise of Spoken Soul." *Stanford Magazine*, October. https://stanfordmag.org/contents/in-praise-of-spoken-soul#:~:text=There%20are%20certain%20things%20I,that%20are%20sometimes%20permanently%20damaging.

Roupenian, Kristen. 2017. "Cat Person." *The New Yorker*, December 4.

Rowles, Dustin. 2015. "The Time a Real PLane Hijacking Was Mistaken For A 'Candid Camera' Stunt." *UPR)XX*, October 24.

Saul, Jennifer M. 2006. "Pornography, Speech Acts, and Context." *Proceedings of the Aristotelian Society (Hardback)* 106 (1): 229–48. https://doi.org/10.1111/j.1467-9264.2006.00146.x.

Saul, Jennifer Mather. 2024. *Dogwhistles and Figleaves: How Manipulative Language Spreads Racism and Falsehood.* Oxford University Press.

Sbisa, Marina. 2007. "Hot to Read Austin." *Pragmatics* 17: 461–73.

Sbisa, Marina. n.d. "Illocution and Silencing." In *Language in Life, and a Life in Language: Jacob Mey—A Festschriff*, edited by B. Fraser and K. Turner.

Scanlon, Thomas. 1990. "Promises and Practices." *Philosophy & Public Affairs* 19 (3): 199–226.

Scheman, Naomi. 1980. "Anger and the Politics of Naming." In *Women & Language in Literature & Society*, edited by S. McConnell-Ginet, R. Borker, and N. Furman. Praeger.

Schiffer, Stephen R. 1988. *Meaning.* Clarendon Pr.

Schow, Ashe. 2020. "Conservatives Self-Censor on College Campuses: Are More Open to Having Liberal Friends." *The Daily Wire*, February 17. https://www.dailywire.com/news/conservatives-self-censor-on-college-campuses-are-more-open-to-having-liberal-friends.

Schroeder, Mark. 2022. "Attributive Silencing." In *Oxford Studies in Normative Ethics Volume 12*, 1st ed., edited by Mark Timmons. Oxford University Press: Oxford. https://doi.org/10.1093/oso/9780192868886.003.0009.

Scoccia, Danny. 1996. "Can Liberals Support a Ban on Violent Pornography?" *Ethics* 106 (4): 776–99. https://doi.org/10.1086/233672.

Searle, John R. 1969. *Speech Acts: An Essay in the Philosophy of Language.* Cambridge University Press.

Smith, Kiona. 2021. "Meet Onesimus: The Enslaved Man Who Saved Colonial Boston From Smallpox." *Forbes*, February 28.

Solnit, Rebecca. 2014. *Men Explain Things To Me.* https://newrepublic.com/article/118555/rebecca-solnits-men-explain-things-me-scourge-mansplaining.

Spender, Dale. 1980. *Man Made Language.* Routledge & Kegan Paul.

Sperber, Dan, and Deirdre Wilson. 2001. *Relevance: Communication and Cognition.* 2nd ed. Blackwell Publishers.

Spewak, David C. 2023. "Perlocutionary Silencing: A Linguistic Harm That Prevents Discursive Influence." *Hypatia* 38 (1): 86–104. https://doi.org/10.1017/hyp.2023.2.

Stalnaker, Robert. 1974. "Pragmatic Presuppositions." In *Semantics and Philosophy*, edited by M. Munitz and Peter Unger. New York University Press.

Stalnaker, Robert. 2002. "Common Ground." *Linguistics and Philosophy* 25 (5–6): 701–21. https://doi.org/10.1023/A:1020867916902.

Strawson, P.F. 1964. "Intention and Convention in Speech Acts." *The Philosophical Review* 73 (4): 439–60. https://doi.org/10.2307/2183301.

Unnsteinsson, Elmar. 2019. "Silencing without Convention." *Pacific Philosophical Quarterly* 100 (2): 573–98. https://doi.org/10.1111/papq.12260.

Vadas, Melinda and Journal of Philosophy Inc. 1987. "A First Look at the Pornography/Civil Rights Ordinance: Could Pornography Be the Subordination of Women?" *Journal of Philosophy* 84 (9): 487–511. https://doi.org/10.5840/jphil198784938.

Waldron, Jeremy. 2012. *The Harm in Hate Speech.* The Oliver Wendell Holmes Lectures, 2009. Harvard University Press.

Waltman, Max. 2021. *Pornography: The Politics of Legal Challenges.* Oxford University Press.

West, Caroline. 2003. "The Free Speech Argument Against Pornography." *Canadian Journal of Philosophy* 33 (3): 391–422. https://doi.org/10.1080/00455091.2003.10716549.

West, Caroline. 2012. "Words That Silence? Freedom of Expression and Racist Hate Speech." In *Speech and Harm: Controversies over Free Speech*, edited by Ishani Maitra and Mary Kate McGowan. Oxford University Press. https://www.jstor.org/stable/2379993.

Wieland, Nellie. 2007. "Linguistic Authority and Convention in a Speech Act Analysis of Pornography." *Australasian Journal of Philosophy* 85 (3): 435–56. https://doi.org/10.1080/00048400701572196.

Williams, Hayden. 2019. "I Was Assaulted at Berkeley Because I'm Conservative. Free Speech Is Under Attack." *USA Today*, March 6. https://www.usatoday.com/story/opinion/voices/2019/03/06/berkeley-conservative-students-campus-college-bias-punch-column/3065895002/.

Wyatt, Nicole. 2009. "Failing to Do Things with Words." *Southwest Philosophy Review* 25 (1): 135–42. https://doi.org/10.5840/swphilreview200925114.

Index

For the benefit of digital users, indexed terms that span two pages (e.g., 52–53) may, on occasion, appear on only one of those pages.